W9-AHM-691

ADVANCED CYCLE TRADING

Cutting Edge Techniques
for Profiting from Market
Tops and Bottoms

AL GIETZEN

IRWIN
Professional Publishing®
Burr Ridge, Illinois
New York, New York

© 1995, Al Gietzen

Originally published as *Real-Time Futures Trading* © *1992*

ALL RIGHTS RESERVED. No part of this publication may be reproduced, stored in a retrieval system, or transmitted, in any form or by any means, electronic, mechanical, photocopying, recording, or otherwise, without the prior written permission of the publisher and the author.

This publication is designed to provide accurate and authoritative information in regard to the subject matter covered. It is sold with the understanding that the author and the publisher are not engaged in rendering legal, accounting, or other professional service.

ISBN 1-55738-881-1

Printed in the United States of America

BB

1 2 3 4 5 6 7 8 9 0

Dedication

To my sons

Darryl
Derek
Randal

Contents

. . .

List of Figures

Foreword

The task which confronts today's investor is monumental. Never before has there been so much unrest in the world of finance and so much volatility in the markets. Effective timing is a strong prerequisite to survival and profit in the investment world. But the task with which the speculator is faced is still more weighty than that of the investor.

Short-term traders must have the ability to implement precise timing. And in this battle against the markets and emotions, only those who are able to achieve effective timing and iron discipline will emerge victorious. The low success rate, which is well known throughout the futures industry, is a strong testimonial to the fact that futures trading is a risky business. While it is generally believed that stock trading is less risky than futures trading, I feel strongly, based on my more than 20 years of experience in both fields, that the majority is wrong in most cases and at most times in both the futures and the stock markets. And this leads to the question, "Why?"

Several lengthy books could be written in response. Even then the answers would prove insufficient. Reality is being interpreted by human beings who perceive events against an internal backdrop shaped by a myriad of factors from heredity, early childhood experiences and life circumstance. The behaviors prompted in different individuals by the same events are often diametrically opposed. News which confirms a bullish predisposition to one trader validates a bearish stance to another.

We trade the way we think. For traders who are able to maintain an objective view of the markets, of their abilities, and of their performance, the lack of an operational and objective trading system may pose no problem. But for the overwhelming majority of the traders, the "seat of the pants" approach (which is commonplace) leads only to losses, frustration and anguish. It is the rare trader indeed who can be successful without objective technical tools as a guide to self-control. And this is the essence of trading systems, timing methods, indicators, charts, computer programs, seasonal analysis cycles, and so on. It is to this end that Al Gietzen offers the book that you are about to read.

In my view, the purpose of any good book about trading is threefold: first, to offer ideas about market timing; second, to illustrate how these ideas are applied in real time; and third, to stimulate thought for additional research. Al has achieved all three goals admirably.

If you expect to come away from reading this book with final answers to cyclical riddles that have plagued traders for many years, then you've set unrealistic goals. But if you're looking for a practical, tradable, workable, and above all, an understandable way of using cycles to your advantage, then you've come to the right place. Within these pages, you will find important answers to the perennial issues of timing in conjunction with cycles. And you'll learn how to apply them in a consistent and objective fashion which will take much of the guesswork out of cyclical timing.

I only wish that I had known these indicators back in 1982 when I wrote the *Handbook of Commodity Cycles—A Window on Time* (Wiley & Sons, publishers). Al has gone well beyond my original work in providing specific timing indicators and analytical methods which will unlock the power of cycles. And in doing so, his techniques will help you overcome the chief enemy of the trader—emotion.

Jake Bernstein
Northbrook, IL

Preface

But as I see it now, as I feel it, I want my visions to come out of my own juices, by my own effort—the hard, ancient way.

I mistrust visions come by in the easy way. . . . the real insight does not come from this.

Lame Deer
Sioux Medicine Man

The trading of commodity futures carries with it the reputation of high risk. But the flip-side of risk is reward. The key is to understand the risk and take appropriate measures to control it. After all, most things in life involve risk; it is only when we act like we're **not** taking a risk that it is dangerous.

This book is an outgrowth of my personal struggle to understand the markets and to develop and adapt technical methods which could outperform all that I was able to find in the literature. But as I used and refined the methods it became evident that the successful trading method was only one piece of what is essentially a three-piece puzzle. A sound methodology must be accompanied by a sound money management system; and there must be an understanding of, and solutions to, some of the key psychological problems that inhibit overall trading success.

As a guide to profitable trading, the book necessarily became more comprehensive and covers all three areas. The combination of the three main ingredients—methodology, psychology and money management—can bring the risks of speculative trading into line with those of other entrepreneurial activities. And with the reduction of risk in this high-leverage business, substantial profits can be made.

The intent is to provide a succinct and thorough approach in each area to give useful and workable solutions. Thus the serious novice can use it as a complete guide to successful trading. The new approach presented, as well as the presentation of the technical foundations of both new and old indicators, can be useful to the professional seeking better methodology. The original analytical approach to limiting losses as part of the money management system can be used by all traders, regardless of methods used.

The trading methodology presented utilizes a new technical indicator that I call "Market Reactivity." It is an analytical indicator that goes beyond the typical use of price behavior alone. It incorporates changes in trading volume and volatility to give a more complete indication of market behavior; and it is then used in conjunction with the inherent cyclical content of each specific market, making it a powerful tool. It has broad applicability to stock and commodity markets and adapts to possible changes in the inherent behaviors of these markets over time.

The calculations required for the indicators, and for the identification of the approximate cycle content, require the use of a computer. The method is adapted for use with standard spreadsheet software so no special software or equipment is required.

For those wishing to use the method without spending the time and aggravation of doing the programming can simply purchase a spreadsheet "template" from the author for specific commodities (see order form at back of book). These are in Lotus 1-2-3 or Excel format for IBM-compatible computers and include all necessary equations and graphics.

I found existing literature on money management in trading limited and even more contradictory than information on trading systems. Besides answering such questions as where to trade, how much capital is needed, how much of an account balance should be used as margin, and when to add to a position, Chapter 4 makes a valuable addition to risk management by providing an analytical approach to determining stop-loss points. It limits risk based on the market behavior (price movement and volatility) rather than arbitrary comfort level or fractions of a guessed potential reward.

A complete demonstration and explanation of trading over a 90-day period of actual data for five different commodities is given. This period was not chosen because the system happened to work well: an arbitrary period was selected, and the same period used for the demonstration of all five commodities. It is in this section where the reader can get information on an application of the method specific to a given market.

The importance of psychological factors is usually the last area appreciated by an aspiring trader. Prior to presenting the technical methods, the importance of these factors is highlighted and some key character traits for successful trading are discussed. The last chapter then returns to the psychological aspects and discusses the key components of trading stress, the common pitfalls experienced by traders, and some suggested ways of dealing with these psychological traps.

The book is of most benefit to those who have at least some familiarity with the futures market, the use of a computer, and an interest in the technical analysis of the markets. The concepts are stated in a concise manner; that is, things are explained only once, so it needs reading in an atmosphere conducive to concentration. Of particular interest to the more inexperienced trader, Appendix A presents an introduction to the futures markets, how they work and who uses them.

It is a complete guide to commodity trading and provides a method that has shown the ability to generate substantial return. Here is an opportunity to examine all the details of a technical trading system and its application before you spend hard-earned money on specialized trading software.

ACKNOWLEDGMENTS

Trading commodities and writing a book are both solitary activities. With no built-in support group in these activities, the support and encouragement of friends and family is paramount, and for their support I am grateful. In particular, thanks to Elaine Blackburn, Roger Kinnischtzke, Jan Winn and Lynn Thompson Winn. Special thanks to my cousin, the psychologist Rose Turner, for her review of the trader psychology, and to Wil Price for his penetrating technical review and expertise as author of many books.

Al Gietzen

Introduction

To fly as fast as thought, to anywhere that is, . . . you must begin by knowing that you already have arrived.

Chiang's advice to
Jonathan Livingston Seagull

Even those who invest and trade in stocks will try to convince you that commodity prices are too volatile and the risks too great. But look at the stock market in recent years. It has been extremely volatile and risky. The principal difference in the risk factor between stocks and commodities is the degree of leverage that is allowed. The cash needed as margin in trading commodities is a small fraction of the value of the commodity that you actually control with the contract. This greater leverage, while adding to the risk, also equates to greater opportunity.

Taking advantage of the greater leverage and making greater profits by speculating in commodity futures requires at least three ingredients: a sound methodology, sound money management, and proper trading psychology. Diligent application of sound principals in these areas can bring the risk of commodity-trading into line with other kinds of investment or income producing activities.

If we're going to be taking risks, we must be sure that we understand what we're doing, act like we're taking a risk, and take the steps necessary to control it. In essence, that is what this book is about. It presents the complete development of a technical market trading system, a sound approach to money management, and discusses some of the key psychological factors that affect the outcome of a trading program.

Development of methodologies for speculating in the commodity markets generally is divided along the lines of "fundamental" versus "technical." Fundamental analysis looks at all those factors in the marketplace that affect the supply and demand, and therefore the price, of the commodity. These are many and complex, and often it is difficult to interpret the net effect on the market.

This book deals with technical analysis. Technical analysis attempts to bypass some of the uncertainty in the interpretation by concentrating on how the market is actually reacting. This is based on the assumption that the net effect of all the fundamentals, as they are being interpreted at large, is what causes the current market behavior. So it is necessary to extract some underlying behavior characteristics that can then indicate what is expected in price movement.

The manner in which fundamental factors affect market prices in the short term is largely because of trader and investor sentiment. Sentiment changes, as well as some of the fundamental factors, are not entirely random. Like so many other things in nature, the price behavior tends to vary in a way that can be described as a complex combination of cyclical patterns. By doing an approximate unraveling of the cycles inherent in the market behavior, and constructing a trading system in harmony with it, we can make timely trades. As is the case with "chaos theory," we are finding the non-randomness in the market behavior and exploiting it.

You don't have to believe that the markets are governed by some inherent cycles in nature. All that is relevant is that the observed behavior can be suitably described in this way, and that we can use this description to better know when to buy or sell to make profits.

A new measure of market behavior called the "market reactivity" indicator is introduced in this book. It is an indicator that combines analysis of the price, the trading volume, the price range (volatility) and the inherent cycle content into one powerful tool. The reactivity indicator, along with its associated "critical ranges," is the principal tool of the trading method developed.

The problem with most technical trading systems is that they lag too far, especially for short-term trades. By the time you get in too late and out too late, you haven't made any money. The system developed around the "market reactivity" concept cuts the "lagging" problem by teaming the indicator with the inherent cyclical patterns in the particular market. This allows immediate identification of short-term trend change and is key to timely entry and exit.

A new, logical and mathematical approach is also developed for determining "stop-loss" points. We know that no indicator system is foolproof. A major challenge of the trader is the effective limiting of losses. The method gives stop-loss points, providing minimum risk consistent with current market behavior. This gives the trader the backup of always knowing the point at which to exit a trade if the price moves against the position. Besides minimizing risk, this alleviates the stress of uncertainty for the trader.

By exploiting the intrinsic characteristics of any given market, the method is not market specific. It can be applied to many different commodity futures, stock indices or to individual stocks. You can trade directly in the stocks, or futures contracts, or their respective option contracts. Nor is the method specific to a given period of time. It is an adaptive technique, i.e., possible changes in market behavior are handled by adjustments in the analysis.

The approach presented both encourages and requires study. Although a relatively simple set of rules defines the use of the indicators, it requires some practice to get good at using the techniques because at times some judgment is required. And, although there may be some black-box computer programs that you can buy which will produce some profit by a purely "mechanical" approach, the belief here is that the added use of our human judgment and flexibility can result in significantly better trading results.

In a basic way, the adaptive nature of the method and the judgment and flexibility factors are consistent with another topic *du jour* in technical analysis, "neural networks." I believe the ultimate neural network is the human brain.

In addition to developing a sound methodology for trading, it must also be recognized that a significant part of successful trading has to do with psychology. In our cultural setting, the concepts of money and winning have as much to do with emotions as with the intellect. The major psychological aspects that determine our ability to make substantial profits are presented as they relate to our trading success.

The methods presented are intended for use with standard spreadsheet computer software. No expensive specialized software is needed.

Yes, the use of a computer is necessary. Anything less rigorous would be bypassing a major tool and would probably not put you into serious contention with the traders who use them.

It is assumed that the reader has a basic understanding of the markets, has perhaps attempted trading, or is, in any case, serious about its pursuit. The minimum level of knowledge required can be obtained by studying the free brochures you can get from your local stock and commodity brokerage house. Some computer savvy is needed for application of the methods, but, of course, you can start learning that right now. The experienced trader can also benefit from application of the techniques presented to improve trading results.

Emphasis is given to the explanation of the foundations upon which the technical system is built. The mathematical formulations are generally straightforward for someone with at least some algebra background. The belief here is that the most successful application of the methods can be made with a good understanding of the methods. The presentation of the foundation of some other "commonly" used technical indicators is also given, along with examples of how some of these are used incorrectly because the original derivation is overlooked.

Even if algebraic equations are a foreign language to you, don't be intimidated. You can simply buy the spreadsheet file for Lotus 1-2-3 (or compatible) with the equations and graphics already built in (see order form in back of book). But challenge yourself to try and understand the approach to whatever extent you can, and then concern yourself with the end result: profitable trading. In return for some effort to understand, and the willingness to use some judgment, you will gain a good understanding of how the markets work and how to trade them profitably.

I have studied many books on technical trading methods where the examples of the method being applied always work well. Authors have a tendency to select data which shows things working out well. Perhaps when *you* try to apply the system to current data, it doesn't work. There is always that disclaimer that says past performance is not necessarily indicative of future results.!

In Chapter 5, you will find a demonstration of the application of the methods for different commodities for a specific 90-day period. This period was arbitrarily chosen and the same period is used for all five of the commodities which will be discussed as examples. There's no picking and choosing of the times when things worked best. Nevertheless, you will learn how profits were made, and how and why the trades were made even though in some cases things got a little messy. (Of course, that disclaimer about future results applies here as well.)

There is a common argument that if a system worked, everybody would use it and the markets would change so that it would no longer work. Not to worry. If there were only a handful of traders and they all read this book, perhaps that would be true. But there are many thousands of traders, and most will already have a system that they prefer. Only a relative handful will ever read this book, and then only a small fraction will follow through and actually use the system. The widespread application of the computer has changed market character, and changes in global communication can change the market; but making this system available will have negligible effect on the markets. It will only affect the profitability of an individual reader's trading program. Go for it!

1

Laying Foundations

■   ■   ■

If you look hard, things aren't as random as everyone assumes.

Persi Diaconis
Stanford University
(professional magician turned statistician)

We've all done it—perhaps when we were younger. On a day of puffy white clouds, we'd play the game of finding the shapes of animals in the clouds. And if you looked for a particular animal, chances are you could find it. Fantasies? Yes, but then, some of the clouds actually *did* have the shape of elephants, lions, bulls, or bears.

It was Henry Thoreau who said, "Dreams are the touchstones of our characters." A touchstone is a criterion, or standard, by which to measure things. So without the dream, we wouldn't set out to find the elephant.

We wouldn't find the inherent rhythms in the behavior of the markets, nor would we pursue the potential profits in using them in trading.

But it should be clear that this is not a whimsical quest. Trading in the futures markets is not something that you can pursue as a hobby to make yourself rich. It has to be taken seriously and requires dedication in getting to know the markets and how the trading system relates to the market. Perhaps the most difficult aspect is getting to know yourself under the pressures, discouragements, and the celebrations of trading. And it can be fun.

1.1 IS THIS INVESTING OR GAMBLING?

Speculative trading of commodity futures is neither investing nor gambling. To better understand what futures trading is, we need to agree on what is meant by investing, speculating, trading, scalping, and gambling. And since each author has his own time frame, we need to know what we mean by short, intermediate, and long-term.

"Investing" and "long-term" go together. Investing is putting your money into an endeavor: income-producing real estate, business, or whatever, where its value is used to generate a flow of revenue, generally with some value added by people and products. Or it can produce revenue strictly for its use (interest) as in various debt instruments (bonds, bills, etc.). The investor is looking for some income stream and/or increased value over time resulting from growth. Generally, the periods of time are from six months to a few years, or more. We'll call this long-term.

Speculating is buying or selling something, usually involving an element of risk, for the primary purpose of making a quick and/or large profit, solely by virtue of a change in its perceived value. Trading is speculating, but with the further definition of being short-term, and is generally done in liquid markets.

Many may argue that speculating/trading is synonymous with gambling. Gambling is a form of speculating where the odds are set (usually against you), and you have little or no control over them; for example, slot machines, lottery tickets, etc. The rule is simple—on the average, you lose. It's a form of entertainment. You have no responsibility for the outcome.

If—by the application of intelligence, objectivity, patience, discipline, mathematics, and a pinch of science—we can influence the outcome, then we can make a transition from gambling to speculating. That transition may seem to be a grey area. A knowledgeable poker player who can compute the probabilities and use good money management to get the odds in his favor may not be a "gambler." Most of all, we must take responsibility for the outcome.

For our purposes, speculating is using a variable over which we have no direct control; in this case, prices, to our benefit by applying those things just mentioned. We will find ways to use the change in the value of investment vehicles, whether it be stocks, futures, or options contracts, to make a profit.

And we will have some control, and certainly the responsibility for the outcome, by applying technical analysis to get the probabilities in our favor. The money we "invest" is not going to pay salaries or build products. It's simply going to be a paper entity which will change in value because of other changing conditions, mostly human sentiment.

In the context of stock and commodity speculative trading, the time scales are usually short to intermediate term. Short means from a few days to a few weeks. Intermediate term means from a few weeks to a few months. We will deal with some sort of cycle where you buy or sell the same vehicle over and over as its value goes up and down. This kind of speculating is called simply "trading."

With the advent of nearly immediate information availability, "day-trading" has become popular with off-floor traders. As the term implies, these are intra-day trades suited to those who need more action, or who are uncomfortable holding positions overnight. The principal disadvantage is that you are dealing with smaller price moves, and commissions become a larger percentage of the trade. It requires a higher win/loss ratio to be profitable.

"Scalping" refers to short-term trading in which one tries to take advantage of short-term reactions in price, usually in volatile markets, perhaps varying from a few minutes to a few hours. This is not recommended unless you're a floor trader.

So what is commodity trading? It's a profession. It's the most basic form of capitalism—buying and selling to make a profit. You can be your own boss with no payroll to meet. It makes no products, has no employees, no suppliers, or sales staff. And since it consumes no natural resources and creates no waste products, it is environmentally compatible.

1.2 THE PRODUCTS AND PRICES

By now, you have studied the various products that have been devised by various organizations or exchanges that are traded in the markets. And whether it's buying and selling used cars or pork belly contracts, the basic process is the same. A willing buyer and seller both agree on a price which they each perceive as value and consummate a trade.

The markets we are interested in are the ones in which there is considerable liquidity, and where we can get good leverage. We want reasonable trading volume, and we want to buy and sell using an amount of cash which is only a fraction of the actual value of what we are controlling.

This cash that we need is called "margin." If we buy stocks, it is like a down payment and ranges from about 30 to 50 percent, and the balance is borrowed from the broker. If we're trading futures contracts we are not actually buying or selling anything, but are simply contracting to buy or sell at a future date. The margin is really just "earnest money," or an indicator that it is a good faith contract. It provides the clearing broker some room for the price to move against you before a negative trade balance occurs.

Margins requirements on commodity futures contracts vary with the brokerage firm, but in no case are they below minimums established by the exchanges. The minimums on most commodities currently vary from about 2.5 to 7 percent of the controlled value with the stock index futures being close to 10 percent.

Options on futures are the right to make a futures contract at a specific price at a future date. These rights are purchased and the amount of cash required is less than the margin on futures contracts.

These are the products and they are traded in quantity at the major exchanges. The basic approach to knowing when to buy and sell is basically the same for all of these products, and the methods presented in this book are applicable for any of them. The most extensive application of the methods has been in the trading of futures contracts, so most of the discussion will refer to commodity futures.

Appendix A provides a brief discussion of who the players are in the futures game, and why.

Let's get back for a moment to the idea of price and value mentioned above. They are not the same thing, at least not always. "Price" is the value as perceived by one buyer at one moment, whereas "value" is the average price paid by many buyers over a period of time. Sometimes people pay too much and sometimes they get a good deal. It is relative to some average accepted price. The markets are a large auction where buyers and sellers are making deals, and the price varies up and down in the vicinity of value; sometimes above, sometimes below, and sometimes at value. A good discussion of price and value is provided by Steidlmayer and Koy.[1]

One thing about people, particularly groups of people, is that they (we) have a great propensity to be short-sighted and to over-react. One year, we're threatened with a coming ice age; the next year it is global warming. But, in fact, studies of global temperatures over the past 100 years show temperatures have cycled up and down, but don't yet indicate any discernible trend. Market prices are controlled by the sentiment of groups of people, and there is over-reaction in both directions. It's wonderful. That's what makes it possible to make money as a market speculator.

For whatever reasons, the sentiment of the traders and investors in a particular market tends to vary in some fairly regular cycles. It is not too surprising. We evolved in a world of cycles: day-night, winter-summer, full moon-new moon, happy-sad, the tides, etc. There is nothing precise about the market sentiment cycles, but they do tend to group into certain lengths or "periods."

Using technical market indicators that are not keyed into some inherent behavior characteristic in the markets is somewhat of a stab in the dark. By using the cyclical tendencies, and observing the price, trading volume, and volatility (as seen in the daily price range), we can calculate trading indicators that show when to buy and when to sell. There are also other important data that can provide us with supporting information. These include the change in contract open interest in commodities, and the advancing and declining issues with their respective volumes in the stock indices.

1.3 WHO SHOULD TRADE COMMODITIES?

Anybody can trade commodity futures. Few can trade successfully. All that is required is some money and an account with a brokerage service. It doesn't require a degree, or certification, or any particular qualifications. An individual makes his own determination whether or not to attempt trading commodity futures for a profit.

Therein lies the reason why the statistics seem so overwhelming against success. Ten percent of the traders make 90 percent of the profits. About 90 percent of those attempting commodity trading lose their money and/or quit trading in the first 12 months. You have to be at about the 90 percentile in terms of ability in this business just to be breaking even.

---

1   *Markets and Market Logic*, Chicago, IL, The Porcupine Press, 1986.

Well, it's probably not as tough as those statistics make it sound. Since no credentials are required (other than some money), there are a lot of would-be millionaires who treat it like a roll of the dice and contribute to the lop-sided statistics. It is easy to make money trading commodities, just like it's easy for a concert pianist to play the piano.

You have to make an investment in becoming proficient. You may even need a certain innate ability. You'll have to study, analyze, devise, withstand tedium, suffer, learn how to lose, be patient, learn how to win, and do some original thinking. Then there's a good chance you'll make some money. A few people make a lot of money. Many more make a comfortable living. Some stay close enough to breaking even that they keep on trying.

You can make a lot of money without putting in the time and effort. You can make $10,000 on the pull of a lever with a $3 investment, but the odds are seriously against it and you can't do it consistently over the long term.

1.4 LEARNING BY EXPERIENCE

By way of example of what may be some typical experiences of the novice trader, I will share some of my personal experiences. My first venture into the high leverage business of futures and options speculation was very successful. I had been developing a screening system for growth stock selection and had followed the stock market behavior for some time. This was all fundamental analysis which is fine for the longer term.

To learn more about technical market analysis, I signed up for a university extension course on stock and option technical analysis. The gentleman "teaching" the class was a great salesman. He was also a broker. The "class" was held in the conference room of the brokerage company's offices. This was really just a sales seminar!

Despite the quality of this instruction, my fundamental analysis had led me to believe that the stock market was poised for a major rally. During the first class, the "instructor" made a lot of references to the Elliott Wave Theory, and dynamically sold the idea that the market was about to make a "giant" up-move and the way to play it was to go long (buy) index "call" options.

Since his definitive, and I believed "expert," statements reinforced my own belief, there could be little doubt. The next day I went to his office, opened a trading account and handed him $15,000 to buy OEX call options. This was on Friday. By Monday, the market began to rally. By Wednesday, I had an $18,000 profit. I was euphoric!

Not only had I found a vehicle which suited my need for immediate results, I had stumbled upon the man who was going to handle this process of getting rich while I went skiing, boating and enjoyed my life.

The next few days we lost some money, but I don't remember how much. Over the next couple of years, I found that I could clearly remember the profitable trades; the losers were always kind of vague. One day, I came off the ski slopes at midday to call my broker. "We" had just made close to $10,000 that morning. This was heady stuff.

Four months later, I was net $8,000 in the hole. Could it be that this wasn't going to be as easy as I thought? I began my search for another broker who knew something more than a vague notion of Elliott waves, cosmic cycles, and gut feel. I found one in Los Angeles who knew a lot of different technical trading techniques. I started him with a relatively small account to see how things would go. He lost $5,000 for me trading stock options in a few months.

The picture began to clarify. I'd just been lucky up front. There still was no easy way to make easy money. Because of my technical background and problem-solving abilities, I decided that making profits in the markets was a problem I should be able to solve, and I set out to do it.

I began my research of technical market analysis while continuing to trade with the original broker, but that wasn't working. He couldn't just do what I asked. After all, he was the expert; he had taught me, right? I would call to make a trade, and he might question what I wanted to do. I would lose confidence in my own concept. How could I know? He was down there with his "hand on the engine," so to speak, with quote screens, speed dialers, etc. All I had at that time was a telephone and a calculator.

Several months later and many more thousands in the hole (many thousands of which represented commissions), it was clear to me that if I was going to make money, I was going to have to do it by myself with no one else's opinions. I had to be the expert and trade through a discount broker who would simply execute the trade.

If you want to trade commodities, you have to be your own expert. You have to learn a system, or develop your own, and you must stick to it. Don't be influenced by other people's opinions. Forget the so-called experts. You are to be the expert.

I continued my research of a broad range of market technical analysis methods. It was time to apply my own scientific background and insight and compile techniques and indicators that worked for me. And whatever the method was to be, it had to out-perform those that were already available and in use.

Even after I had compiled a collection of indicators, some borrowed and some original, I learned that to really know them, to be able to use them consistently and correctly to trade profitably, was like being able to read a musical score. It takes time, practice, commitment, practice and finally, confidence.

When you are confident that you know what's happening and are following your system, the stress of trading subsides. You don't think about money; the technical aspect of the trade is everything. Then the money takes care of itself. Now you can sit down to play, and even a difficult score is enjoyable instead of stressful.

If this makes sense to you, and you're willing and able to dedicate the time and effort, then you can choose to trade commodities and do it successfully. And doing it successfully means going beyond making substantial amounts of money. It means enjoying doing it, and it means the satisfaction of mastering the skills.

The methods presented in this book are not intended for a consistent, low, or even moderate rate of return. Compared to what we're after with this method, the rates of return on CDs or treasury bills are zero. And after inflation, that's about it. We are after substantial returns like doubling annually or better. It takes diligent effort and acceptance of a higher degree of risk. And, of course, we'll be satisfied with less if that's how things work out.

Keep in mind that a sound methodology is only part of this endeavor. It has been observed that a group of traders being given specific winning recommendations did not achieve a success rate that was obviously above the norm.[2] Why did they go wrong? That is the other major part of this endeavor—the psychology of trading. In the remainder of this chapter, we will look at some of the underlying principles of the technical method and the psychology.

1.5 THE BASIC PREMISE

The foundation that underlies the trading methods developed in this book is that the market price behavior can be described approximately as a

---

2   Chisholm, Michael, *The Mega-Trade Method*, Brightwater, NY, Windsor Books, 1987.

combination of simple cycles of differing periods and amplitudes acting more or less independently of one another. This is not a new idea, but one that has been studied extensively. The new idea is the manner in which the premise of cyclicality is shown to apply and, most importantly, the indicators that are developed to exploit the cyclical nature.

It may come as a surprise to some that many commonly used trading indicators are built on this same foundation, e.g., market momentum, the relative strength index (RSI), even multiple moving average (MMA) systems. The interval for computing momentum and the length of the averaging periods must be selected in accordance with some inherent cyclical tendency of the market if they are to produce positive results.

The actual existence of specific time cycles in market price behavior is not universally accepted. It is argued that being able to see these cycles is akin to seeing elephants in the clouds, i.e., if you look for shapes that resemble a specific shape, chances are you will find them. Imagination works wonders.

For our purposes, we need not argue one way or another. The only thing of importance is whether or not the assumption of specific cycles allow the construction of a methodology that works and makes consistent good profits. The mathematical or physical authenticity of cycles is secondary. But be open minded and read on. It is shown that combining a few simple sine waves of the observed periods and amplitudes allows the reproduction of hog prices or the Dow Jones average remarkably close to the actual data. You'll see that a search for "non-randomness" in the market data shows that it exists to a high degree.

But, like most things in art and nature, there is randomness. A 15-day cycle is not always 15 days. That's fine. We're looking for a tool to improve our odds, not an absolute. Putting too much "faith" in any indicator can lead to big disappointments. Realize that different cycles dominate at different times, and, in strongly trending markets some cycles cannot be tracked at all for a few cycle periods. Occasionally (fortunately seldom) they undergo a phase shift. That's why some more sophisticated mathematical procedures such as Fourier analysis are not all that useful.

The objective is to develop some techniques to find cycles that repeat with some regularity, i.e., where the standard deviation of the period length is less than about 20 percent of the period. We don't just trade when we think the cycle is at the top or bottom; we construct good indicators to use as tools to track the cycles and the indicators tell us when to make the trade.

1.6 USING THE CYCLES

If we can show that the price behavior can be well represented by a combination of repetitive cycles, then there is a valid basis for pursuing methods of determining when these cycles are topping or bottoming. This will be shown by expressing the price behavior in analytical form as a function of time. The generalized mathematical formulation of this approach is provided in Appendix B.

The simplest form of a smoothly oscillating cycle is conveniently expressed as the trigonometric sine function. We will assume that each of the component cycles can be described as a sine wave, and we will assume mathematical linearity, that is, that the total effect of all cycles combined is given by simply adding the cycles.

We know, for example, that the wave equation describing the motion of water waves is a mathematically linear equation. This means that its many different solutions, each with a different amplitude and wave length, can be added together to get a new solution to the wave equation. This simply reflects the physical fact that water waves can superimpose on one another. Similarly, the behavior of a market price as a function of time can be described as a summation of cycle solutions for different wavelengths (periods) added to an underlying mean value.

The number of terms (cycles) used in the analytical form depends upon the cyclical content of a given market, the degree of accuracy sought, and the time scale of interest (long-term or short-term). For example, consider the price data for live hog futures given in Figure 1-1. Detrending analysis of hog data over the years has shown repetitive cycles of about 120 days, about 35 days, and a very short cycle that varies between about 4 and 8 days. Being interested in trading cycles in this range we can see if the price behavior can be represented adequately by these cycles.

The analysis shows that, even if we ignore the shortest cycle, the price behavior can be represented remarkably well with just two harmonic terms giving the 35- and 120-day cycles. We can represent the hog price as:

$$P = \text{Average over the longest cycle} + \text{individual cycles}$$

$$P = \overline{P}_{120} + A \sin T_1 + A_2 \sin T_2$$

where: A is the amplitude of each cycle, and
         T is the time period function.

Figure 1–1   Live Hogs—1989

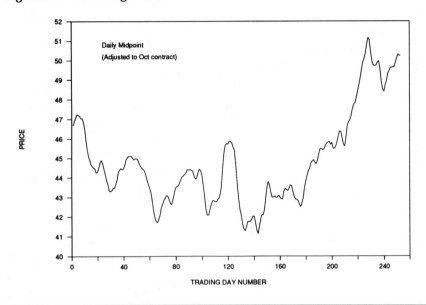

Figure 1–2   Live Hog Cycles—1989

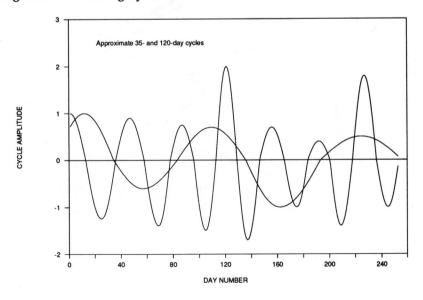

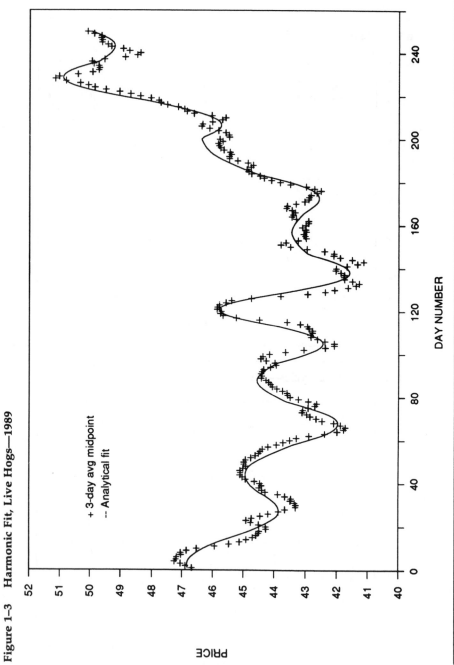

Figure 1-3 Harmonic Fit, Live Hogs—1989

+ 3-day avg midpoint
-- Analytical fit

Figure 1-2 shows the curves given by the two harmonic terms for the two cycles. The actual periods and amplitudes were taken from detrending analysis. Simply arithmetically adding these two cycles to the centered 120-day average of the daily price midpoint gives the curve shown in Figure 1-3. The actual data is also shown for comparison. Clearly, there is cyclical content here that, if tracked with a suitable indicator, can pinpoint trading opportunities.

Similarly, a more complex example can be given for the stock market. Detrending analysis identifies stock market cycles of approximately the following lengths (periods):

1	5-8 days	
2	12-16 days	3 weeks
3	25-32 days	6 weeks
4	45-60 days	10 weeks
5	85-110 days	20 weeks
6	225-275 days	52 weeks

The Dow Jones Industrial Average should then be represented as a long-term average plus the six harmonic terms:

$$P = \overline{P}_{250} + A_1 \sin T_1 + A_2 \sin T_2 + A_3 \sin T_3 \ldots A_6 \sin T_6$$

Again, as an example of what some of these simple harmonic cycles look like, Figure 1-4 shows the 6-, 10- and 20-week cycles for the stock market for the first half of 1988. The resulting fit using these and the other cycles listed covering the entire year is shown in Figure 1-5, showing both the calculated results (solid line) and the actual data. This was a particularly volatile period, and one might expect it to be difficult to reproduce analytically. The results are seen to be very good, again showing that using a few simple cycles to describe the market is a valid approach. Similar good agreement is obtained for other time periods and other markets.

Does this mean that the future can now be predicted, and we can make good trades every time? No, it means that the data can be fit with a simple series of sine waves. The problem with reality is that the amplitude can vary significantly from one period to another, and the periods of each cycle are not always the same. In these examples the periods and amplitudes were adjusted to the apparent actual values after the fact.

Figure 1-4 Example Stock Market Cycles

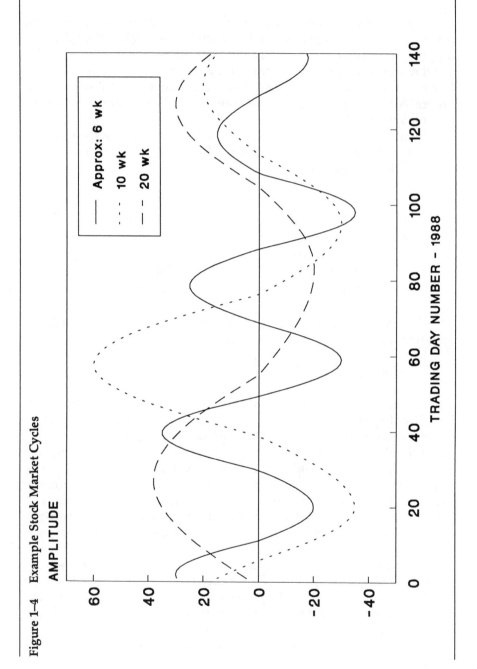

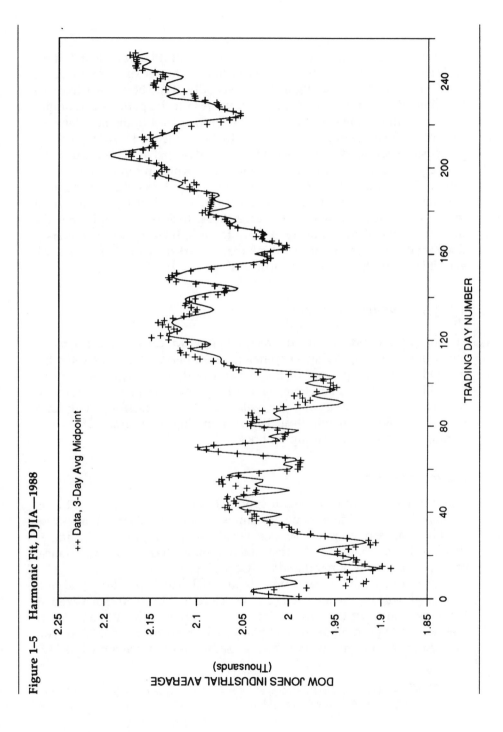

Figure 1-5   Harmonic Fit, DJIA—1988

++ Data, 3-Day Avg Midpoint

DOW JONES INDUSTRIAL AVERAGE (Thousands)

TRADING DAY NUMBER

Doing the analysis does two important things, however. First, it establishes the validity of the cyclic behavior and the use of these cycles for the development of a trading method. Secondly, it can be a predictive tool to a limited extent, i.e., by using mean values for the periods and amplitudes we can get some idea of what to expect, at least in the near term.

What becomes of real importance to trading is the knowledge of the principal cycles which can be used to describe the behavior of a particular market. This allows construction of indicators which provide timely indication of tops and bottoms, even on a short-term basis. But it is good to remember that this, as other technical trading tools, is using an analytical technique to describe what the market does. It does not imply that the market is controlled by, or necessarily follows, these cycles. The market does what it is going to do. To think that a market "should" do what we expect is a trap that the trader must avoid.

1.7 SOME PSYCHOLOGY

Having set a foundation for the methodology, we turn to another major factor in successful trading—psychology. Jake Berstein[3] suggests that the method is only 20 percent of a successful trading strategy. He may be biased because he is a psychologist, but his point is well taken. A successful method is essential, but you will not trade successfully without a proper psychological mind-set. Before pursuing a program of futures trading, I recommend reading his book.

The Inner Game

Those of you involved in certain sport activities are familiar with books written about the "inner game" of tennis, skiing, etc. These books stress the importance of concentrating on what's happening inside you rather than just the mechanics of the required motions. It has to do with balance, or a "centeredness," a mind and body condition.

In trading, this "inner game" is an intellectual, psychological and emotional balance, the importance of which cannot be overemphasized. It is the most difficult to learn, and is usually learned only after a series of mistakes have been made. It can't really be learned from a book, but you can become aware, and with an awareness, master it much more quickly.

---

3   *The Investor's Quotient: The Psychology of Successful Investing in Commodities and Stocks,*
     New York, NY: John Wiley & Sons, 1980.

It is nearly impossible to trade in a purely objective manner no matter how mechanical the method. We're dealing with money. In our culture, money is tied up with success, failure, hope, fear, greed and a myriad of psychological/emotional factors. When you apply your judgment to any matter, your action depends on how you perceive the situation. And your perception is strongly influenced by emotional/psychological factors.

In a broad sense, successful short-term trading relies upon exercising good judgment and remaining flexible in our thinking to be aware of all alternatives available at a given time. To achieve that, we must have four key qualities:

Discipline
Patience
Courage
Objective Perception

Place these four characteristics into your mind now so you can begin to think about and develop them as you proceed through the rest of the book. After taking you through development of the method and some trading examples, we will come back to the trader psychology in Chapter 6 to explore some of the typical traps that can limit your trading success. For now, consider the following definitions and discussions.

Discipline

Discipline is a state of order based upon submission to rules. The trading system must always be followed. It is easy in trading to submit to other emotional responses, e.g., fear, hope, greed, etc. We don't even realize that we're doing it until we are behind on a trade, or have missed a trade, because we thought we knew better than the indicators and the rules tell us. Larry Williams,[4] one of the most successful contemporary traders, does not attribute his success to having a great system, but to being a good system follower.

Perhaps one reason why it is so easy to get trapped into "fudging" on the system rules is that we know they are not always right. There is a strong temptation to try to do better, or to hesitate out of fear because we think that the system is wrong or that we don't want to wait for it.

---

4   *The Definitive Guide to Futures Trading*, Brightwater, NY: Windsor Books, 1988.

It is not that there isn't value to intuitive inference; it is just that experience has shown that, particularly in off-floor trading, intuition may not be operating properly. There are too many other emotional responses clouding the picture. The system is sometimes wrong, but on the average it's right. It has been studied, modified, tested, and modified until overall it's the best you can do.

Patience

The American Heritage Dictionary says that patience is "the capacity of calm endurance," and in trading, "endurance" is the operative word. You must wait until the market tells you what to do. When you are anticipating a trade and the days wear on without the proper trade signal from your indicators, it gets very difficult to endure.

One of the most difficult problems that the trader has to overcome is not waiting for the indicators to tell him what to do. There is a strong tendency to anticipate the trade—to feel certain that you can get in at a better price now than if you wait. After all, the time frame is right for a cycle bottom, the market seems to be finding support, and we know that technical indicators generally lag. Sometimes it may be right to jump ahead, so the tendency gets reinforced. But too many times, you'll risk big losses while the market finishes its move.

So add patience to your discipline and wait. It is better to get in on the move a little bit late than to have to get out at a loss and start over. In the system developed in this book, the short-term trading indicator will give you a timely trade—sometimes even when you wait for it you may get in too early.

Courage

Every trade you enter exposes you to risk as well as potential reward. There is a considerable degree of uncertainty each time you pick up the telephone and commit hundreds or thousands of dollars to a trade. It takes courage—the ability to face risk with confidence and resolution.

Courage allows you to be persistent, which is a key to successful trading. You will take losses in the course of trading. It's part of the game. If you follow all the rules, these losses will be small relative to the gains. But a series of even small losses can be discouraging. Sometimes you may make a mistake and sustain a bigger loss. And it is at these times that there is a strong feeling of wanting to give up. This is where you must summon your courage, and when the indicators and rules say to make a trade, you pick up the phone and do it. Remember that, when trading, your system rules are the highest authority.

Objective Perception

Our actions are not necessarily determined by things as they are, but rather, as we perceive them to be. In other words, the things that we experience are interpreted by our mind and are subject to some degree of filtering. Biases get applied. In trading, we will occasionally interpret what is happening in the market, and what our indicators are telling us, in accordance with some existing belief. These are usually "preconceived notions" of what is going to happen.

A common misconception regarding technical trading is that it is a method of foretelling the future. It is not. All we know is what has already happened and what is happening now. We are simply counting on pattern recognition and pattern repetition, and the indicators tell you whether or not that is occurring. Everything else regarding the future is preconceived notions.

Objectivity—the ability to remain uninfluenced by emotion, surmise and prejudice and to be aware of only that which has factual reality in our trading system—is essential. Objective perception is the ability to evaluate each day's data in a totally unbiased manner; you have no idea of what will occur next. For most of us, that is difficult.

1.8 WHOSE METHOD IS RIGHT?

Apparently there is an ego involvement in writing a book; hence, there is a tendency on the part of authors to suggest that his/her psychology or methodology is "right" or "correct." A surprising number of the works that I have read on investing or trading suggest that the reader should forget any other ideas they may have had and accept those presented.

From a standpoint of using a particular strategy for trading, it may be advantageous to limit oneself to some specific concept or approach in order to avoid confusion. But none of these are necessarily "right" or even "best." It has to be a system that you understand and feel comfortable with.

Study different authors and trading systems, stay current on new techniques being developed, and preferably build or expand your approach based upon some breadth of understanding. Although the end result of technical methods development may be some set of rules, the objective is to develop and understand the basis for the concepts because the success or failure in applying the rules depends on some understanding of the foundations.

And, of course, the reason for doing all of this is to make substantial profits. But try to make it your objective to follow the system, not to make money. The money will take care of itself. In spite of all the promotional hoopla on publications and trading books which people sell to make money, the chance of getting rich quick is unlikely. It is possible. More importantly, by some diligent effort and careful money management, you can grind out some good profits. And, as you learn how to grind out these profits, you'll learn how to get rich.

2

The Technical
Concepts

■   ■   ■

*The reason science works is because it studies an ordered world that
can be known by an ordered mind. Why the world is ordered is unknown. But that it is ordered seems undeniable.*

Heinz R. Pagels
The Dreams of Reason

Methodologies for trading in the stock or commodity futures markets are generally divided along the lines of "fundamental" versus "technical." This book concentrates on technical analysis. It is
not concerned with price chart patterns, but applies analytical relationships to the data that is readily available about the markets.

Fundamental analysis looks at the factors in the marketplace that affect the supply and demand, and therefore the price, of the stock or commodity. These are many and complex, and it is often difficult to interpret the net effect on the market.

Fundamental analysis of a stock, for example, might include evaluating a company's balance sheet (price/earning ratio, price-to-book value ratio, assets/liability, return on equity, revenue trends, etc.), as well as the more subjective factors of potential product competition, management capability, and so on, to make a judgment of anticipated future stock price.

Similarly, for a commodity, evaluations of the fundamental factors would include weather considerations, projected acreage or herd size, labor problems, political interference, shipping costs, currency exchange rates, and so on.

Technical analysis attempts to bypass some of the uncertainty in the interpretation by concentrating on how the market is actually reacting, on the assumption that the net effect of all the fundamentals, as they are being interpreted at large, is what is now causing the market behavior. It assumes that the factors affecting supply and demand are influencing the current trading behavior (price, volume, open interest, volatility, etc.) relative to past behavior. The anticipated future price direction can then be inferred from the factors describing the current trading behavior, and from the extraction of some underlying repetitive behavior characteristics that have occurred in the past.

An important factor affecting price behavior which is included in technical analysis is sentiment. Sentiment is a measure of human perception; that is, how the buyers and sellers perceive the effects of the fundamental factors. As you may have observed in short-term market behavior, sometimes good news is good news, and sometimes it is bad news.

So there are two basic premises underlying technical trading systems for stocks and commodities. The first is that any available information on conditions that may affect the price, is already affecting the price. The second is that the price and the derived trading indicators will repeat, in some approximate way, the patterns that have occurred in the past.

The first premise means that we do not need to concern ourselves with news of fundamental factors. We only need to concern ourselves with how the market is behaving. The second premise leads us to analyze the past repeated patterns of market behavior, in conjunction with some derived indicators, and to use these repeated patterns with the expectation of a similar outcome in the future.

For successful short-term timing of trades, some form of technical analysis is a must. For successful long-term investment, fundamental analysis may be a must. For short-term trading, awareness of underlying fundamental factors affecting price can be helpful in explaining market behavior, but generally **after** the fact.

The technical concepts presented here concentrate on the development of a new methodology designed to be adaptive to market behavior and to give more timely trade points than other published approaches. It is an evolutionary approach in that it builds upon and is supplemented by concepts previously applied. The concepts which serve as a basis for, or are supplemental to, the development of the "reactivity" indicator system, are also presented. You may wish to continue your research of the many other approaches presented elsewhere to broaden your understanding or to find other tools which appeal to you. After all, trading style is a personal trait.

It is worth keeping in mind that when studying technical analysis, give more credence to an author with some technical background. For all of the information that is available, there is a great deal of misinformation.

All of the equations used are presented, hopefully in an understandable and usable form. If you have a technical background and the use of Greek letters doesn't mean it's Greek, the generalized mathematical form of most of the equations used is presented in Appendix B.

2.1 THE IMPORTANCE OF THE TIME FACTOR

Nearly all markets exhibit some relatively regular cyclical behavior, whether it is because of seasonal factors, sentiment, phases of the moon, or whatever. Many traders who do not monitor the existence of regular cycles are using analytic methods which were developed with a built-in dependence upon a given cycle length for their effectiveness. The concepts of momentum, moving average, stochastics, relative strength (RSI), and various over-bought or over-sold indicators all depend upon a proper selection of time period, usually a cycle length or one-half cycle length.

Most users of these methods fail to realize the built-in assumption of a cycle length and therefore misuse, or fail to adjust the parameters to get proper use of the indicator. For example, why do you use a 14-day period for RSI, or why use a 30-day moving average? These periods were found to be optimum because of the half-cycle or cycle length. The use of momentum, for example, is meaningless without also specifying a proper half-cycle period.

2.2 THE REAL MOMENTUM

So-called market momentum will be the first technical indicator discussed because the concept serves as a basis for the development of the market reactivity indicator. The simple momentum is also a useful short-term timing device to use in conjunction with the reactivity.

For those of you with a background in the physical sciences, we'll note that "momentum" as used in market analysis is no momentum at all, but more akin to velocity. It is a measure of the amount of change in price (or other variable) over a given period of time. So, in a mathematical sense it is a "slope."

It is graphically depicted in Figure 2-1 and mathematically stated as:

$$M = \frac{Y_2 - Y_1}{X_2 - X_1}$$

If the Y-axis is price and the X-axis is time, then it becomes an average change in price per unit of time; for example, if $Y_2 - Y_1$ is $0.10 and $X_2 - X_1$ is 10 days, then the momentum is $0.01 per day. A similar down slope is -$0.01/day. This simple concept is useful for timing trades if used properly in conjunction with cycles.

We will use this to construct an oscillating indicator by computing its value each day, over the same period of time, and its values will vary over some range around zero. The oscillator value will increase and become positive as prices increase, and it will turn and go negative as prices decrease.

Since the momentum indicator for a given cycle length will always use the same time interval, the denominator is a constant. It is a normalizing factor and can be removed from the equation, so a momentum can be expressed as:

$$M = Y_2 - Y_1$$

Figure 2-2 shows an idealized price/time behavior with a cycle period of 28 days. If the momentum is computed each day over a period of one-half the cycle length of 14 days, the resulting momentum oscillator will be shown by the solid line in Figure 2-3.

A typical point on this curve is that given over the period between A and B (Figure 2-2) as:

$$M = B - A = 27.8 - 25.0 = 2.8$$

Figure 2-1 Computing Momentum (Slope)

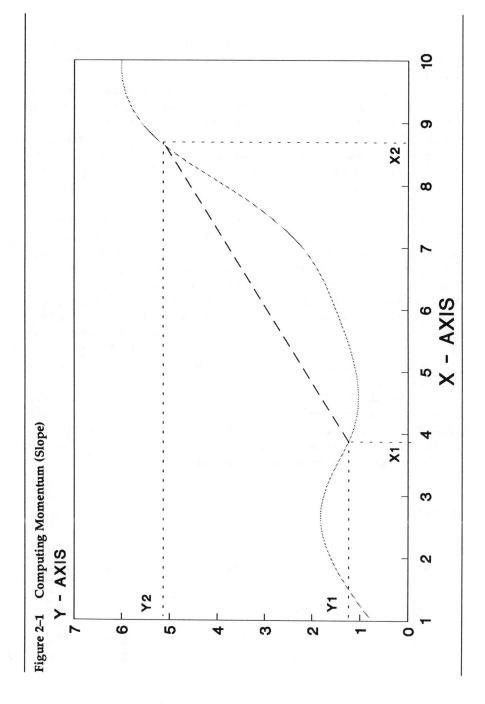

Each day the momentum value is computed over the same period, it is always the current price minus the price 14 days earlier (1/2 the cycle length).

Looking at the price curve (Figure 2-2) and the 14-day momentum curve (Figure 2-3), you can see that the time to buy is at a point just as the momentum turns up, day 38, and the time to sell (and sell short) is at a point just as the momentum turns down, day 51. The key is that if the period over which you take the momentum is half the cycle period, the momentum turns as the price turns. That is the basic concept for the advantageous use of the momentum indicator, it provides a means for timing the turn of the cycle.

Assume that on the same idealized price behavior you arbitrarily choose to use a 21-day momentum. The resulting oscillator would be as shown by the plus signs curve in Figure 2-3. The turns in this oscillator significantly lag the turns in the price so it would not be a good indicator. Table 2-1, below, compares the trade signals obtained using momentum periods of 14 and 21 days. The profits obtained from using the too-long 21-day indicator are only a small fraction of those obtained with the indicator length adapted to the cycle content of the given price behavior; in this case, 14 days. To carry this further, you can see that a 28-day momentum on the idealized 28-day cycle would not oscillate at all; it would be a constant small value.

So it is obvious that if the price cycles have any sort of regularity, talking about momentum is meaningless unless a proper time period is also specified. And taking the buy/sell signal as the point where the momentum oscillator crosses zero, as has been suggested by more than one author, would clearly not be an effective trading indicator.

Table 2–1

	14-day			21-day		
	Day	Price	Profit	Day	Price	Profit
Sell	23	27.5	—	28	26.2	—
Buy	38	23.7	3.8	42	25.6	0.6
Sell	52	28.8	5.1	56	27.5	1.9
Buy	66	25.0	3.8	70	26.9	0.6
Sell	80	30.1	5.1	84	28.8	1.9

Figure 2–2   Computing Momentum

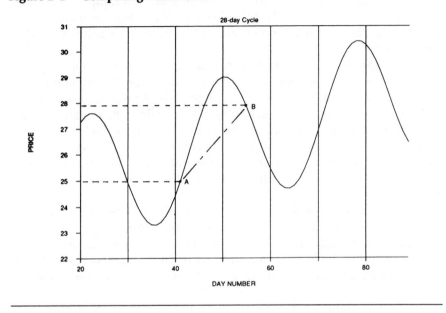

Figure 2–3   Idealized Price Cycle

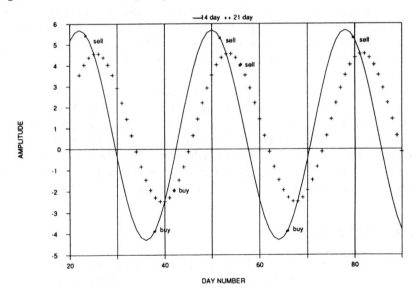

As discussed earlier, most markets can be described by the combination of a number of cycles of different periods. We can compute a momentum for each cycle independently to keep track of where they are, and we can use the shorter cycle momentum to fine-tune entry points to trade a longer cycle.

If things always worked like this idealized case, we could stop here and go trade using momentums. But this is not to be. To use momentum effectively, we need to know what sort of cyclical behavior exists. So we will need some tools for determining the specific cyclical nature of the price of a given stock or commodity. And we can't just go look them up because, although data is available on most commodities, there is considerable disagreement on what the cycle content is depending on what techniques are used to decipher the cycles, and these cycles are not invariant in time.

There are other problems with the use of momentum. Probably the most significant is that it is the opposite of trend-following. It is good for finding turning points and therefore will tend to get you out of a trade at the first little pullback, even in a strongly trending market. There is truth in the old adage that "the trend is your friend" that we don't want to violate.

There is also a need for some techniques to eliminate scatter in the raw data which can lead to spurious buy and sell signals.

These are solvable problems. We can use some relatively straightforward techniques to find the cycles with strategic use of averages as filters. We can address the trend problem by incorporating additional market information; most importantly, volatility and trading volume. And we can eliminate scatter in data by using a specific type of average for a specific purpose.

Since averages come into play in significant ways, both in the methods discussed here as well as in many other technical methods, we will take a close look at different types. These include simple averages, weighted averages, exponential averages, centered averages, and trailing averages. One interesting thing we will find is that the most commonly used average in market analysis, the trailing simple average, has the least basis for use and will not be used at all in the reactivity method.

2.3 A JUMP AHEAD

Commodity traders do have a tendency to jump ahead. What happened to the patience we just talked about in Chapter 1? It's not just to satisfy those of you who like to skim the last chapter before reading a book. It is good to have a sense of where this is leading, hopefully to provide motivation to get through the sometimes tedious technical development. It will also provide an opportunity to look at some real data and see how the technical "stuff" is going to benefit. And in jumping ahead, it will just be assumed that you already know about some of the things covered later.

Figure 2-4 shows the daily high and low range of price for wheat futures in late 1987 and early 1988. The first notable feature is that the open and close data is not included. One early discovery I made was the over-emphasis on closing data (daily, weekly, whatever). It is just one point in a continuum of time. For the most part, it is used just because it is convenient. And with few exceptions, the opening price doesn't add much information. The opening number has no trading history whatsoever.

Highs and lows are of interest in determining "daily range" which is an important piece of data. A simple average of the high and low gives the midpoint. When representing the price on a given day (or week or month) by a single number, the midpoint is a better representation than the close. In this respect, I agree with W. D. Gann.

Breaking years of tradition, the analysis will use range and midpoint and in many cases the price charts in this book will simply show the "channel" defined by the daily high and low.

Another point is that "time" in trading is only the time when the markets are open. Since "value" is price weighted by trading volume; from a technical standpoint, value cannot be influenced when there is no trading. The time scale on the charts presented is the number of the trading days, where the trading days are simply numbered in succession from the beginning of each year. Weekends and holidays don't count.

By further examining the data in Figure 2–4, there would seem to be considerable randomness and somewhat of an upward trend. By using averages as filters to "detrend" this zigzagging data as explained further in Section 2.5, we find a high degree of regularity. By simply subtracting a 29-day centered moving average from a 9-day average, shown in Figure 2–5, a regular cycle emerges with a period of about 30 trading days (Figure 2–6). We see that there is a considerable degree of non-randomness.

This wheat cycle averaged 29 days between 1985 and 1989 with a standard deviation of only three days, meaning that roughly 80 percent of these cycle periods fell into the range of 26 to 32 days.

If one were to use a momentum indicator to trade this cycle, we could choose a proper momentum interval of about half the cycle length. To pick up the shorter of these cycles, choose a momentum period just

Figure 2-4   Wheat Futures Price

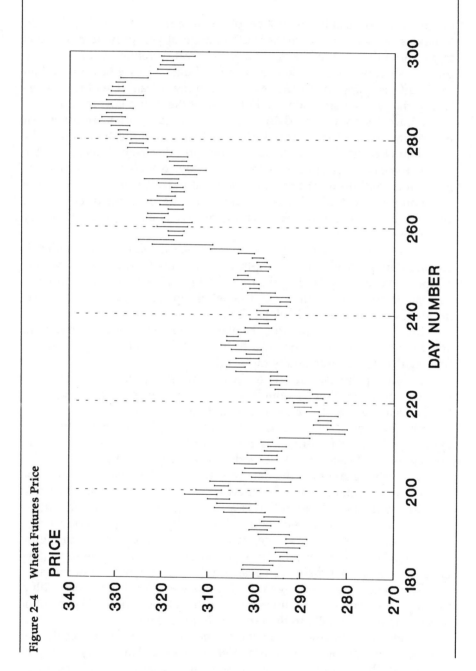

Figure 2–5   Wheat Price Averages

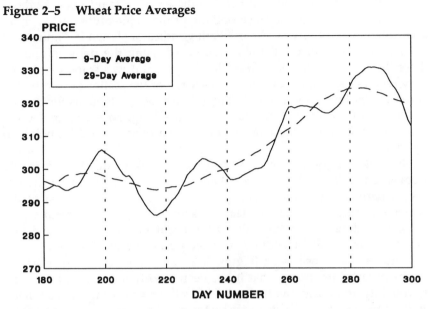

Figure 2–6   Wheat Detrend—29-Day Cycle

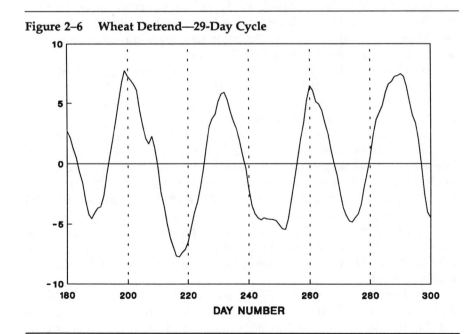

under half the length of the short end of these cycles; in this case, 12 days. It reacts a bit early and allows smoothing of the momentum data with an exponential average, giving the oscillating indicator shown in Figure 2–7.

This momentum oscillator is computed using the daily midpoints where the trailing price data (the 12-day-ago data) was smoothed by an 8-day centered average. This eliminates some of the scatter caused by the shorter cycles. So then you simply buy (close short, go long) as the oscillator turns up from the bottom, and sell (close long, go short) as it turns from the top. Compare these turns with the corresponding price points in Figure 2–4.

It works nicely, but there is still more work to do. You probably discovered that the "sell" on day 264 and "buy" on day 275 or 276 did not make a particularly good trade. This kind of problem is typical of the momentum oscillator and can lead to some disappointing results in a strongly trending market. It is solving this problem that leads to the development of the "market reactivity" oscillator and its critical ranges.

The reactivity oscillator (Figure 2–8) is a cycle-following indicator like the momentum, except that it has been modified to account for market volatility and trading volume. A "critical" range is computed so that a significant penetration of this range by the oscillator brings in special rules to hold the position to the next lower top of the indicator, or to close the position, but not reverse. Therefore, the long position entered on day 245 would be held until day 288, or closed on day 264 and re-entered on day 275, resulting in a profit of about $0.35 per bushel.

The 25- to 30-day cycle on wheat shown in Figure 2-6 is actual data, but the cycle is not always this regular. It makes for good illustration and you can see that knowing what the cycle content is and how to exploit it can be a powerful tool in speculative trading.

Let's examine these wheat trades again from the viewpoint of psychological factors. Although it is hard to experience in the abstract when looking at the whole picture in these graphs, consider that you bought a modest position in wheat on day 244, say four contracts (20,000 bu.) at $2.96. You have watched this trade carefully each day for three weeks (15 trading days), and you have a paper profit of about $4,000. You've seen that profit top at over $5,000. The reactivity indicator is clearly above the critical range by day 258, indicating that you should hold the position. But now in the next few days you see it top again and then pull back as the indicator turns down.

Remember that days have gone by, not minutes. Days and nights. You wake up early in the morning thinking you better take what you've got. Try to visualize yourself in the situation and see what kinds of feel-

Figure 2-7 12-Day Momentum—Wheat

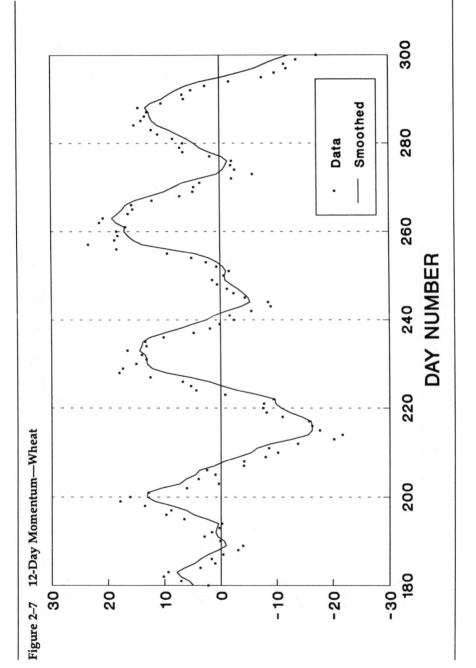

Figure 2-8 12-Day Reactivity—Wheat

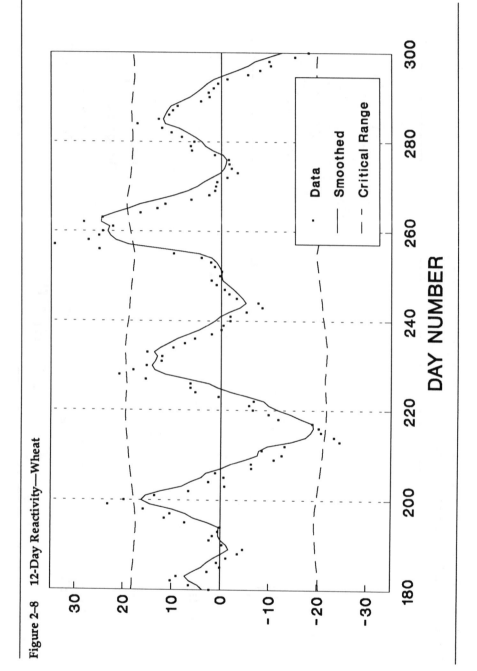

ings you get. Remember that each day you really don't know what's going to happen next. The price may drop so your profit drops to $3,000. Can you stick by the rules? Can you stay with your trade?

In this case, it wouldn't have mattered much if you got out and back in later, but chances are you would have left a gap and spent commissions. It is this sort of psychological test in actual trading situations that leads most traders to do less than their methods allow.

2.4 THE MANY USES OF AVERAGES

In just the single example above, we used two different types of averages in two different ways; simple and exponential, for detrending and for data "smoothing." Averages are also used directly as indicators. This is not an effort to over-complicate a simple concept, but the use of averages in market analysis is extensive, and they should be properly understood. Averages are used to smooth data, detrend data, and as indicators. Still many "market analysts" know only about trailing averages and apply them over arbitrary periods.

Discussed below are simple averages, weighted averages, and exponential averages. Market analysis is generally concerned with a continuum of data, but obviously only a finite number of data points over a specific period of time are included in an average. Depending on where the average number is placed (graphically) to represent the time period, the foregoing types can be used as trailing, centered, or sometimes displaced. I know one trader/analyst who uses a displaced, trailing average.

The Simple Average

Almost everyone is familiar with the simple average. For a set of numbers, you simply add them up and divide by the number of numbers. For just four numbers, the average is:

$$A = \frac{N_1 + N_2 + N_3 + N_4}{4}$$

In market analysis, we are generally averaging a series of numbers, such as price, over a number of intervals (hours, days, weeks) in a period. We want to take this average at the end of each new interval. So the average over the period is just moved along one interval at a time (moving average).

We can simplify the computation of the average and avoid having to add up all the numbers each time by using the recursive technique; i.e., subtracting the first number (oldest) and adding the last (newest). For the next interval, the example above becomes:

$$A_{new} = \frac{N_1 + N_2 + N_3 + N_4 - N_1 + N_5}{4}$$

or since the first four numbers in the numerator were already added for the previous average, A_{old}, we can multiply the old average by four, add the newest number and subtract the oldest and again divide by four:

$$A_{new} = \frac{4A_{old} + (N_5 - N_1)}{4}$$

When taking the average over a long period, i.e., for many intervals (hours, days, etc.), this last formulation is much simpler to compute than re-adding all the numbers each time.

The Weighted Average

A weighted average simply means you consider some numbers in the set that you are averaging to be more important than others. It is similar to a simple average except you multiply each number by a "weighting factor," and then divide them out again. In the simple average, each weighting factor is assumed to be one, so you divide by the number of numbers, which is the sum of the weighting factors. The weighted average is expressed as:

$$A_w = \frac{w_1 N_1 + w_2 N_2 + w_3 N_3 + w_4 N_4}{w_1 + w_2 + w_3 + w_4}$$

In market analysis you may believe, for example, that the most recent data is more important than older data and therefore use weighting factors which progressively increase as the data gets more recent. Or perhaps you want a price which represents a week better than either the midpoint or the close. You take a weighted average by multiplying each day's midpoint by that day's volume, and then dividing out the total volume.

There may be other special purposes for which you may wish to experiment with weighted averages. Generally, weighted averages are not recursive and would almost certainly require use of a computer.

Trailing vs Centered Moving Averages

It is important to understand that a simple average is only representative of the data in the period when it is applied (or graphically plotted) at the center of the period. Therefore, the availability of the last point in a centered moving average always lags the data by 1/2 the period. For example, a 14-day centered average computed on day 70 includes data for days 57 through 70 and is the average for day 64.

Common usage of moving averages in market analysis is to use them as trailing averages where today's average is that for the past N days. This is done for convenience and timeliness and works as a smoothing device.

Figure 2–9 shows a comparison of trailing and centered 14-day simple averages. You see the response of the trailing average lags; i.e., when the index turns down, the average turns down several days later. At any point in time the values are different. As a smoothed representation of the actual market behavior, the centered average is correct. Therefore, when using averages to represent past data, for example, for studying data for detrending of cycles, you must use centered averages. A trailing average will be misleading.

When doing analysis which uses past data points, such as for a momentum, some scatter in the indicator data can be removed by using a short centered average over a period equal to a known shorter cycle.

The Exponential Average

The so-called exponential moving average is not really an average at all, but rather a mathematical expression of a filter. It has become known as an average because averages are used for the same function—that of filtering the higher frequency variations from market data. This particular mathematical form of filter is very useful in market analysis because it is recursive and simple to calculate, and it is forward weighted, i.e., it gives more emphasis to recent data.

The name comes from the way in which the response to previous data in the series is included. The exponential moving average theoretically includes all previous data with exponentially decreasing weight. Each successively more distant term is multiplied by a fraction raised to a successively higher exponent (that is, multiplied by itself more times),

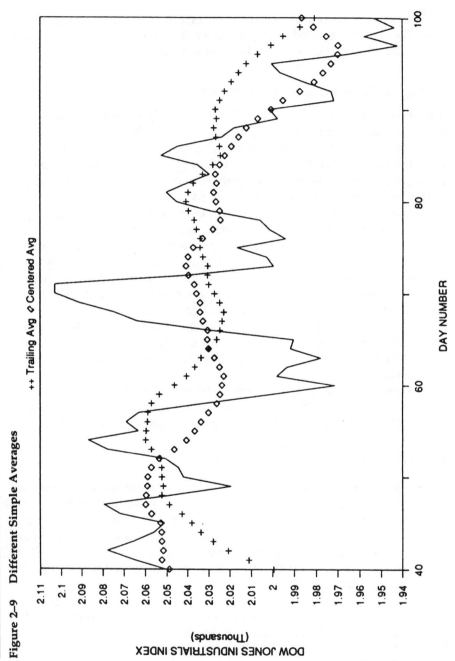

Figure 2-9   Different Simple Averages

++ Trailing Avg ◇ Centered Avg

DAY NUMBER

DOW JONES INDUSTRIALS INDEX
(Thousands)

making its contribution exponentially smaller (see Appendix B, *The Exponential Average*).

In its recursive form it can be stated quite simply. The new average is a fraction times the new data sample added to one minus the fraction (its complement) times the old average. The fraction is called a "smoothing factor" (which we will denote by the Greek alpha, α) and the calculation can be written as:

$$EA_{new} = \alpha P_{new} + (1-\alpha)EA_{old})$$

For example, if the old exponential average is 14.0, the new data point is 16.0 and the smoothing factor is 0.2, then:

$$\begin{aligned} EA_{new} &= 0.2 \cdot 16 + (1 - 0.2) \cdot 14 \\ &= 3.2 + 11.2 \\ &= 14.4 \end{aligned}$$

Another way of thinking about it is that it adds to the old average a fraction of the difference between the old average and the new data point. In this example we added 0.2 times the difference of 2.0 and added it to 14.0. This form is the same equation as given above, but rearranged as:

$$EA_{new} = EA_{old} + \alpha(P_{new} - EA_{old})$$

This is the form that will be used in this book.

For a graphic example of the difference between a simple and an exponential moving average, refer to Figure 2-9. This shows the Dow Industrial Average, a simple 14-day trailing average and an approximately equivalent exponential average with a smoothing constant of 0.15.

In both cases these are plotted as trailing averages, that is, the average is plotted at the end of the 14-day period. The simple average is not as sensitive to price variations in choppy markets because of its equal weighting of all data, and its response to changes is more delayed. You can see that the exponential average is more responsive to the most recent data.

Because its response is not so delayed, the trailing exponential moving average is more representative of the centered simple average. It can also be shown that for values of alpha significantly less than one, the exponential average can be related to the simple average by choosing the smoothing factor as:

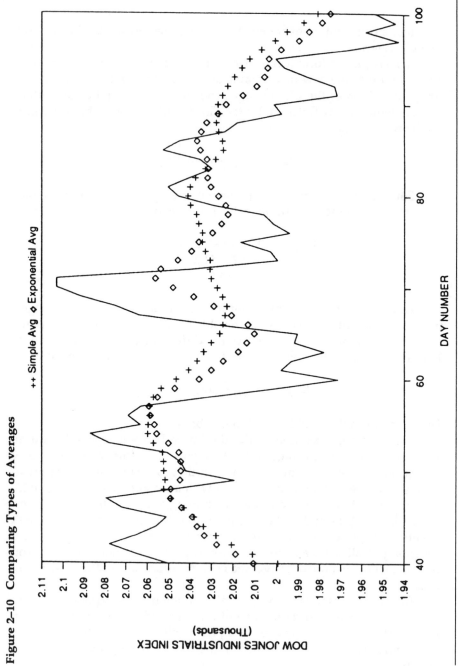

Figure 2–10 Comparing Types of Averages

++ Simple Avg ◇ Exponential Avg

DOW JONES INDUSTRIALS INDEX
(Thousands)

DAY NUMBER

$$\alpha = \frac{2}{m+1}$$

Where m is the number of intervals in the period; i.e., the length of the moving average. So for an approximate equivalence to a 14-day centered simple average, which does not lag by 1/2 the period, use a smoothing factor of

$$\alpha = \frac{2}{14+1} = 0.13$$

As a smoothing device for trailing data, the use of the exponential trailing average is preferred because its forward weighting is more representative of the current behavior.

Averages as Indicators

There are a number of trading techniques in the literature which use turns in various averages as buy and sell signals. One of the most common is the use of the crossing points of trailing averages of different lengths, the so-called multiple moving average system. My comparative studies of these and other similar techniques show them to be either too slow in their response or too erratic to trade satisfactorily for all market conditions.

There is one average indicator technique which does work reasonably well and can be used as a confirming indicator even with the reactivity indicator system. That is the convergence/divergence of multiple moving averages. In this case, we want to use a trailing average so we use exponential averages and select smoothing constants for two periods which differ by at least a factor of two.

Since a shorter term average, i.e., using a larger smoothing constant, will follow the market index more closely than one using a smaller constant, one can expect that the difference between the two would grow larger as a strong trend developed and smaller as the trend slowed and/or changed direction. This is illustrated in Figure 2–11 which shows actual wheat future prices and two different exponential smoothing curves corresponding roughly to 8-day and 25-day periods.

By examining the curves, you discover that the distance between the lines of the "faster" average (smoothing = 0.2) and the "slower" average (smoothing = 0.08) narrows or widens in a responsive fashion as the short term price trend changes.

If we subtract the slower from the faster we obtain the oscillator shown in Figure 2–12. The point at which this divergence of averages changes direction should be taken as the trade point.

In actual practice, particularly for short-term trading, it's not entirely satisfactory because the fluctuations in the indicator can make it difficult to determine whether it is a turning point or not. And one must always keep in mind that when looking at the charts "afterwards," things can seem terribly obvious, whereas at the time, being completely blind as to what the next data point will be, fluctuation in the divergence can lead to a lot of mistakes. Nonetheless, when used in conjunction with other indicators, this can be a useful tool in trading.

The smoothing factors to use are somewhat arbitrary but should differ by at least a factor of two. The values used should be selected in accordance with the time cycles of interest for trading. As was the case with momentums, you want to chose a smoothing constant equivalent to 1/2 the cycle length.

Again, as with momentums, it can be useful to track more than one divergence. For hourly data on stock index futures, for example, I use a 0.1 and 0.05 divergence in conjunction with a 0.05 and 0.02 divergence. These indicators correspond roughly with the 14-day and 28-day (100 and 200 hr) cycles.

2.5 DETRENDING - FINDING THE CYCLES

We have shown that a high degree of success using the trading indicators developed is based upon the ability to describe the behavior of a particular market price as a combination of additive cyclical patterns. Then we must have some fairly rigorous methods for determining what these cycles are for a given stock or commodity. It is not sufficient to look at a price chart and count the days between apparent cycle bottoms unless there is only one dominant cycle. Since there are usually two or more operative cycles, they interact; sometimes reinforcing, sometimes canceling, and the apparent cycle tops and bottoms are misleading.

We find the cycles mathematically by a process called "detrending." This term comes from the fact that we are separating the shorter term variations from the longer term trend. This is a process of "filtering" which allows isolation of a specific cycle length. What constitutes a trend depends upon your reference time frame. A trend to a short-term trader is "chop" to a long-term trader. "Trend" will be the resultant price direction

Figure 2–11   Wheat Futures Midpoint and Exponential Averages

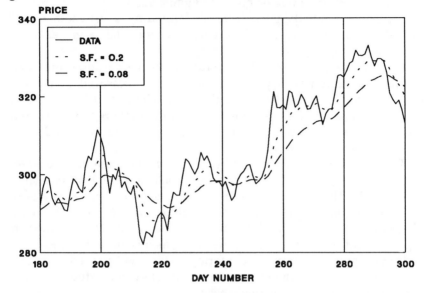

Figure 2–12   Average Divergence Oscillator

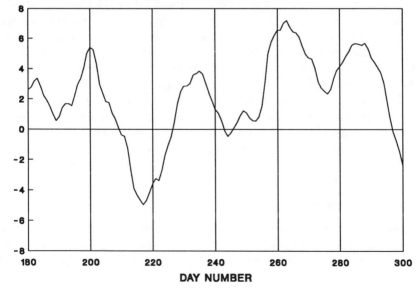

caused by the cycles longer than the one in which we are currently interested, no matter what cycle length is being analyzed.

Since averages make good "filters," detrending is just another application of averages discussed in the previous section. The particular type of
average used is a centered, simple average.

Each cyclical pattern which is useful for trading purposes must show
some reasonable consistency. This consistency is measured by the variation in the length of the period of the cycle. The period is the time between cycle tops or bottoms. Most of the time, cycle bottoms are more
regular than tops; consequently, periods are generally measured as the
time from bottom to bottom.

There are methods for finding cyclical content in data that are mathematically more rigorous than the process explained here. Fourier analysis
is an example. They don't give superior results, however, because of the
degree of variation in the period and amplitude that can exist in market
cycles, but which are still useful in trading. The judgment factor in examining the data is important. That's the part which is art, not science.

Determining the various cycle periods which will be used to describe
the price behavior is somewhat of an art. It takes some study, but with
some practice it becomes relatively easy.

Taking an average of the price data over a particular period of time
smooths out the cycles which have periods equal to, or shorter than, the
length of the moving average. The result exhibits only the longer term
cycles, or the "trend." If we then remove this trend by subtracting the
average from the raw data, what remains is the shorter term cycles oscillating around zero. We can further analyze the remaining shorter term
data to separate a specific cycle. The centered moving average serves as a
simple, yet powerful tool in separating cyclical wave patterns.

Since the period over which we take the averages depends upon the
cycle length that we are looking for, it is a repetitive process. It is necessary to first estimate a cycle length by examining the data, and detrend for
that cycle. Fortunately, if the first guess is anywhere close to an actual
cycle in the data, the second guess will yield the desired results.

Simple Sine Waves

Illustrating this process further, recall from the earlier discussion (Section
1.6) that we are going to assume that the price behavior over time can be
described by an additive series of sine waves of differing periods and

amplitudes. For a simple sine wave of period, P, oscillating around zero, a plot of the moving average over the same period will at each point be zero, resulting in a straight line eliminating the wave. In this ideal case, the average is a perfect filter. For a mix of cycles of differing periods the average is not a perfect filter. It does a good job of smoothing out cycles shorter than about two-thirds of the period being averaged. Fortunately, in describing market data composed of a number of different cycles, periods are such that this condition is almost always met.

So, a moving average of period, P, will smooth out all cycles of period, P, as well as all cycles with shorter periods. The result is the contribution of only cycles with periods greater than P. For example, Figure 2–13 shows an imaginary stock index which has cyclic components of about 6 days, 28 days, 50 days, and a longer term trend. The 28-day centered moving average, also shown on the graph, removes the 28-day and shorter cycle components leaving a clear 50-day cycle and the longer trend.

The detrending of the idealized stock index shown in Figure 2–13 is shown in Figure 2–14. The 28-day detrend is the result of subtracting the 28-day average from a six-day average. The 50-day detrend is obtained by subtracting the 50-day average from the 28-day average. The detrend waves are always curves oscillating around zero no matter what the amplitude of the data. Scaling becomes simple since there are no longer any trends.

There are some interesting things to notice about these examples. If you just examined the data (Figure 2–13), you might get the idea that there was a cycle of about 40 days. Or if you examined the 28-day average, you would find the 50-day cycle but you would place the bottoms at about day 30 and about day 80, when the detrended cycles in Figure 2–14 show the bottoms at 37 and 87.

It is also apparent that there is not necessarily an integral relationship between cycles of different lengths, that is, a 50-day cycle is not necessarily two 25's. Also the bottoms and tops don't coincide. You can see that a fairly rigorous evaluation is necessary to get an accurate picture of the cycle content.

Although, there is a cycle content in the data shown that is exactly 28 days, the 28-day cycle detrends are not exactly 28 days apart. This is due to distortion caused by the combination of waves and the fact that averages are not perfect filters. The average length over many cycles will be close to 28 days.

Figure 2–13   Example Index Data

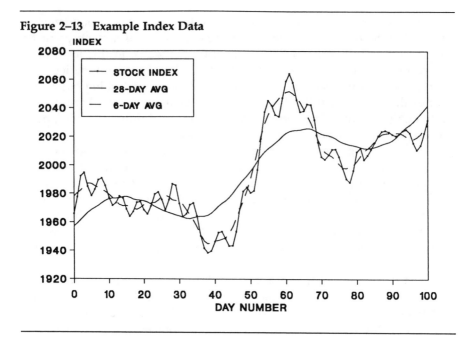

Figure 2–14   Cycle Detrend

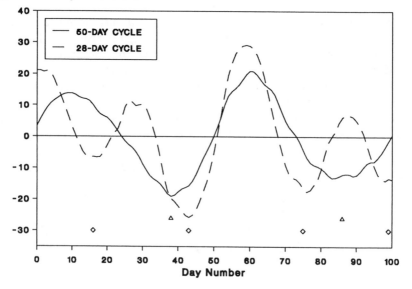

Real Data

So much for theory with simple sine waves. Even then, the average is not a perfect filter, and the combined waves produce distortions. Actual price data can sometimes be difficult because of cycles whose periods you can't determine, and because even the cycles that you can find tend to have some variation, sometimes significant. You will recall, however, that this concept of detrending was introduced back in Section 2.3 with real data for wheat—Figures 2–4 and 25.

Don't be discouraged. Remember, we don't need precision. We are only looking for a cycle which is repetitive within a range suitable for construction of an oscillator for timing our trades. Usually a cycle whose periods have a standard deviation of about 20 percent or less are fine. We only need to establish a "window" in which a turn is likely, and let our oscillator tell us when it is happening.

It is worth reiterating that for detrending purposes, the moving average value is taken at the center of the period. While for a single pure sine wave, it doesn't matter whether you use it as a trailing or centered average; for a composite wave in a strongly trending situation, use of a trailing average will definitely be misleading.

A fairly straightforward example can be provided with the weekly data for live hog futures (nearest contract) shown in Figure 2–15. As noted previously, we are using only the mid-point of the week's range. The weeks are numbered arbitrarily and cover the period from late 1983 through 1986.

In this case, a visual examination can provide a good idea of the weekly cyclical behavior. The dominant cycle is seen to be between 20 and 30 weeks. A 25-week detrending of the data is shown in Figure 2–16. We can subtract the 25-week average from the raw weekly data to give the somewhat jagged curve shown by the solid line. The cycle is seen better if the 25-week average is subtracted from a 7-week average (which eliminates the 7-week cycle) as shown by the curve marked by plus signs. To smooth the detrended cycle curve, and to more accurately represent the cycle period and amplitude, the detrend of a cycle is computed by subtracting from the average over the next shorter term cycle period.

Although the cycle period is variable, it is clearly apparent and assists in trading shorter term cycles in the direction of the trend. It actually averages about 26 weeks and bottoms twice each year, generally in the spring and fall.

The behavior of a given cycle tends to be distorted by longer length cycles. It is common that a cycle period will be extended or shortened at tops and bottoms of dominant longer cycles. Occasionally, a cycle may

Figure 2–15   Live Hog Futures—Weekly Midpoint

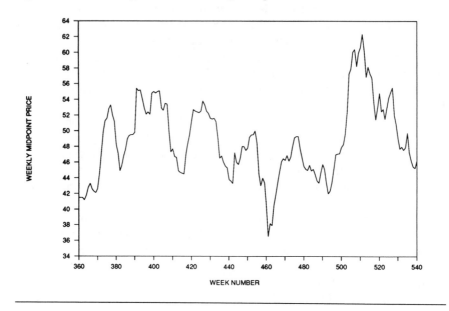

Figure 2–16   Live Hogs—25-Week Cycle

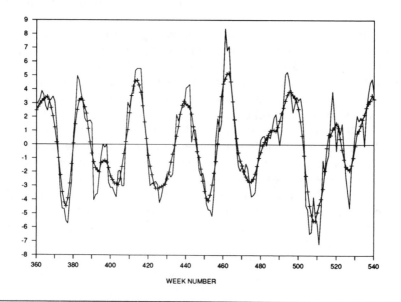

slip a half of a period (as seen around week #490 in Figure 2–16) at major tops or bottoms of longer cycles, usually when more than one longer cycle is bottoming concurrently.

Some cycle theory proponents argue that the cycles describing (or described by) the price behavior in markets are quite precise, always exhibiting the same period. It is believed that the apparent distortions in the periods between bottoms is caused by the interactions of other cycles not identified. This may be true. Further examination indicates that the weekly hog behavior can be described as a combination 7, 12, 40 and 52 week cycles. But when the use of a 26-week cycle is so apparent, there is no need for further complication. It is best to use the simplest combination of cycles that provides tradable consistency.

It is interesting to note that there is a cycle content in the weekly hog data that averages about 40 weeks, and that interaction of the annual cycle, 52 weeks, with the 40-week reinforce every 4 to 6 cycles to produce the 3-1/2 year (180-week) cycle lows.

Further study is encouraged. However, keep in mind that our objective is to profitably trade future contracts. If using a 25-week cycle, or whatever works for the market you're trading, allows reaching that objective, then also developing a definitive theory of the harmonic behavior of a given market is mostly academic.

It's perhaps a question of whether you believe the markets are "governed by" some intrinsic cyclical phenomenon, or whether we are simply using cycle analysis as a tool to describe a fairly random process. Certainly, we can stay more flexible by assuming the latter.

Cycles are not always integral parts of other cycles as some proponents argue; i.e., a 30-day cycle is not necessarily two 15's, or a 45-week cycle is not 3 of 15 weeks. In most markets, there is a tendency for this to occur, and when concurrent bottoms or tops do occur, the better trading opportunities result. Harmonic analysis shows that the behavior is more properly described by allowing that cycles are not necessarily concurrent. A top on a shorter cycle may occur right at the bottom of a longer cycle.

As an example of detrending a more complex cyclical content, we will look at copper prices. The price data for copper futures for 1989 are shown in Figure 2-17. Except for a long cycle of about 100 days, the cyclical content is not readily apparent by visual examination.

The best approach to detrending is to start with the short cycles and work progressively toward the longer cycles. This quickly removes the irregularities in the data which then makes the longer cycles more apparent. The longer term averages are then subtracted from the short-term averages to isolate the individual cycles.

Examining the price data reveals some kind of short cycle which appears to be somewhere between five and ten days. The length of the average that is used is not critical. The first attempt will show the cycle, the periods between bottoms can then be measured and averaged, and the second attempt will give the desired result. To eliminate some scatter, the first average taken will be just three days.

Taking an eight-day average and subtracting it from the three-day gives the result shown on Figure 2–18. Only a portion of the year is shown to expand the time scale. Given the seemingly random short-term chop in the price data, this cycle is reasonably regular. Reading off the distances between the cycle bottoms and taking an average reveals that the cycle does average about eight days. This will make a good cycle for timing of trades for trading a longer term cycle.

It would not have mattered much if the average used for this first detrend was anywhere between six and ten days. The resulting cycle would have averaged about the same duration and second average of eight days could have been taken. This process is straightforward on spreadsheet software and is discussed in more detail in Chapter 3.

Again looking at the price data (Figure 2–17), you see that there is an occasional cycle of about 15 to 20 days. Simply choosing 20 days for the next average and subtracting it from the 8-day average will reveal a cycle with an average period of about 18 days. Taking the 18-day detrend will appear as shown in Figure 2–19. This cycle is not regular and is of fairly small amplitude. Considering that this cycle length is marginally short for trading based on the use of daily data, the search continues for a longer tradable cycle.

Clues to the cycle periods that we want to look for can be gained from visual examination of the data, as we did above, and also from the shorter cycle behavior. The 8-day cycle, for instance, particularly if examined over a longer length of time than shown in Figure 2-18, reveals larger amplitudes about every 30 to 40 days. Taking a 35-day detrend (subtracting a 35-day average from the 8-day average) reveals a cycle which averages about 32-34 days (shown for the entire year in Figure 2–20) and has good amplitude for trading. The period is somewhat more variable than we would like, varying from about 26 to nearly 40 days, but it makes a tradable cycle when followed with the reactivity indicator.

This process can be continued for longer term cycles. The key cycles for short-term trading have been discovered. Application of these cycles to actual trading is presented in Chapter 5.

Figure 2–17 Copper Futures, 1989

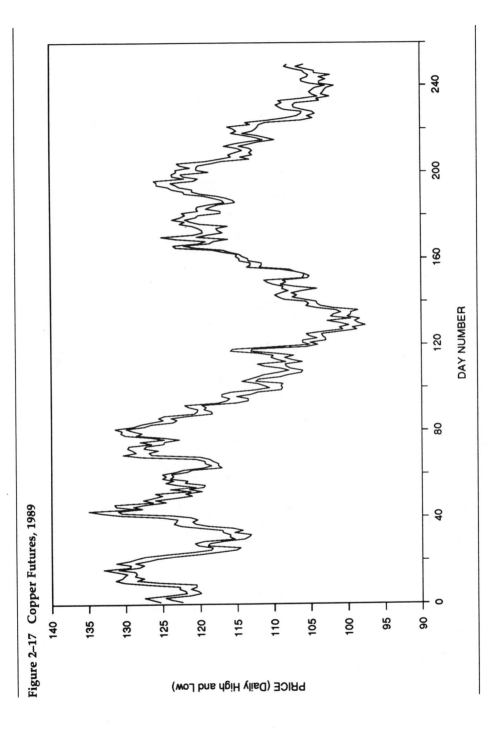

DAY NUMBER

PRICE (Daily High and Low)

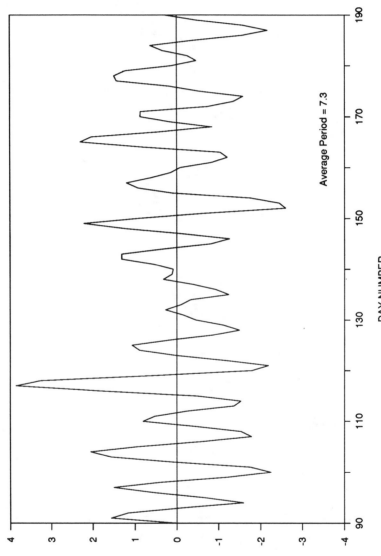

Figure 2–18 Copper Detrend, 8-Day

DAY NUMBER

Average Period = 7.3

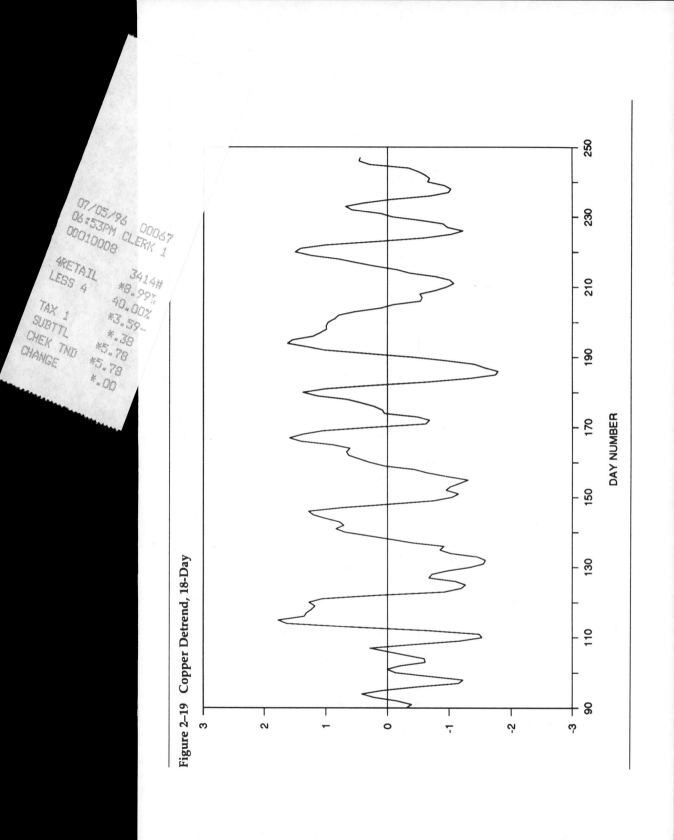

Figure 2-19 Copper Detrend, 18-Day

Figure 2–20 Copper Detrend, 32-Day

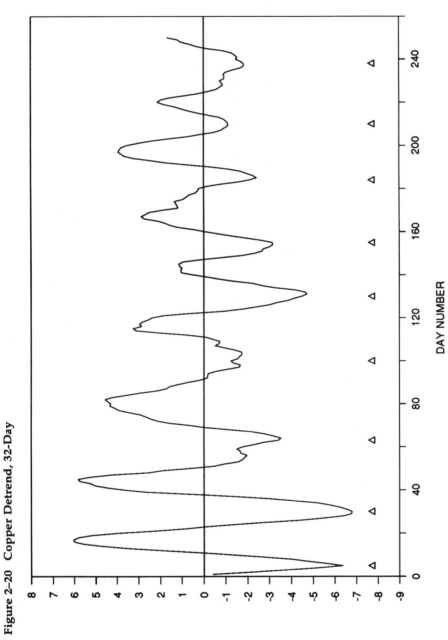

DAY NUMBER

2.6 THE REACTIVITY FACTOR

Most conventional methods for market trading focus almost exclusively on price behavior; specifically, how price varies with time. This includes all of the various charting techniques, moving averages, relative strength, momentum, etc. Sometimes trading volume is considered at least qualitatively as an adjunct, but generally not quantitatively.

The market is spinning out significant information about itself in other ways. Only some of this information is available to off-floor traders in the form of published data. The stock market has the broadest range of readily available data beyond price. From the daily investment journals, you can obtain volume, range, issues advancing, issues declining, advancing volume, declining volume, broad averages, narrow averages, industry group averages, new highs/lows, etc.

But examine the commodity data: price, volume, and open interest. That's about it! So it is necessary to manipulate this sparse data in ways that extract the most usable information about market behavior.

The notable exception to the exclusive use of price in popular trading methods is the market logic or Market Profile™ approach developed by Steidlmayer[1] and popularized by Jim Dalton. This method utilizes a time, volume and range relationship to establish "value" around which "price" is varying. It is a sound approach, but limited to certain markets where the "market profile" information is available, and it is somewhat specialized and requires specific database tie-ins and display software.

The market reactivity indicator provides a way to use the range and volume information in combination with the cyclical behavior we have already established. And we want to do it in a readily achievable, integrated, and quantitative fashion.

Incorporating Trading Volume

The next variable beyond price and time generally considered is the trading volume. Logically, it seems that changes in trading volume would indicate something about market conditions. Yet, it is difficult to find sound quantitative evaluations in the published literature that is of much use for short-term trading.

Some of the qualitative concepts about volume are actually misleading. The idea that "real moves are accompanied by high volume" is popular, but generally that high volume is likely to occur in about the last half

---

1   Peter Steidlmayer, *Markets and Market Logic*, Chicago, IL, The Porcupine Press, 1986.

of the price move and may be highest toward the end. This is not an effective trading tool.

It can be argued that volume should replace the time variable; that is, it's not a question of how much time went by during the certain movement of price, but rather how many contracts, or shares, were traded. This is an argument that was put forth effectively by Richard Arms.[2] And in the "market logic" approach, it is the number of trades at any given price that establishes value.

You can also examine the cyclical behavior in terms of the trading volume between cycle bottoms. Certain stocks exhibit a cyclical behavior as a function of volume which is a more regular cycle than can be found in the time behavior. Merrill Lynch is one example which for many years had a regular cycle of about 18 million shares.

Trading volume is also useful as a component in estimating the money flow into and out of commodity markets. This is discussed in Section 2.7.

Incorporating Price Range

Range is simply the amount of price movement within a given time period—the difference between the high and the low of the period. The daily and weekly highs and lows are common ways of reporting price behavior.

The range is a measure of volatility and also indicates the strength of trends. It can indicate how easily the price is being moved by either buyers or sellers. However, the significance of range is best seen in conjunction with the amount of trading volume from which it was produced.

One of the best ways I have found to visually integrate the price and volume variables is that presented by Arms. Each time period is represented as a box on a chart plotting price as a function of volume. The height of the box is defined by the high and low price of the period, and the width by the volume of trading in the interval. A typical plot of the Dow Jones Industrial Average using a daily interval is shown in Figure 2–21.

This visual depiction provides considerable information not evident from a conventional bar chart. For example, notice that as the market bottomed at around 1950 and began the rally, the volume was light. The major move day (day eight) of the rally was on moderate volume. Heavy

---

2   Richard Arms, *Volume Cycles in the Stock Market*, Homewood, IL: Dow Jones Irwin, 1983.

Figure 2-21 Dow Jones Industrials—Range/Volume

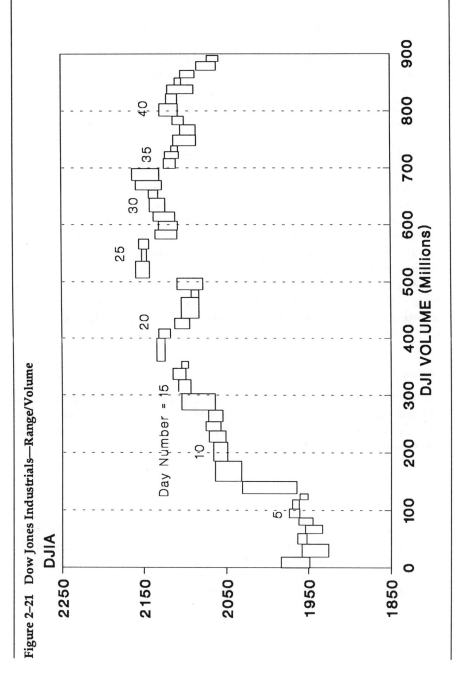

trading began around 2050 (half the move), and the heaviest volume occurred at the first top.

Examining that first top (day 18), we see two important symptoms.
The price range of the day leaves a gap, and the day is flat; i.e., large
volume and small range. This is a classic topping pattern, and this type of
gap is called an "exhaustion gap." The second top is made by a large
exhaustion gap followed by small range over the combined volume of the
next three days (24–26). A sure-fire shorting opportunity. And in conjunction with the cyclical indicators, you would see the third top as a great
opportunity to add to that short position.

The combination of range and volume can obviously provide information about the market. The important parameter is the relative shape of
the box as expressed by the ratio of height and width; not just the range or
the volume. A high aspect ratio; that is, large range on small volume,
indicates prices are easily moved in that direction. **Price** is leading **value**.
This is seen on day eight in Figure 2-21.

As the market consolidates, the boxes become more square as buying
and selling pressures tend toward balance. Day 18 has a low aspect ratio
indicating a close balance of buyers and sellers and provides the indication of a market top.

Measuring Market Reactivity

Just "eyeballing" the range-volume chart is interesting, but what we need
is to quantify these effects and incorporate them into the trading indicators. We have a quantity, the aspect ratio, which is the range, R, divided
by the volume, V:

$$\text{Aspect ratio} = \frac{high - low}{volume} = \frac{R}{V}$$

The characteristic range and volume will be different in different
periods of time and for different markets. We need to answer the question
"What is today's ratio compared to the usual ratio?" We can "normalize"
the range and volume by dividing by the average values for the recent
past to calculate a comparative aspect ratio, f, as:

$$f = \frac{R/\overline{R}}{V/\overline{V}}$$

where: R = range

V = volume
$\overline{R}$ = average range over recent past
$\overline{V}$ = average volume over recent past

The aspect factor will range around 1.0 and indicates the "trendi-ness" of the market. You can see that a larger than usual range for usual volume will make f larger than 1.0. Values of f larger than about 1.4 indicate strongly trending markets, and values much less than 1.0 indicate consolidation. It becomes a measure of market behavior.

By incorporating this aspect factor with a cycle indicator to show when a strong trend is developing, or in progress, we can tell when a short-term cycle reversal is not a good trade. As seen earlier, the so-called momentum indicator is a useful trading tool if the interval is selected to correspond to specific cycle lengths. It works well in non-trending markets to pick highs and lows. It gets you into trouble, however, in a strongly trending market where the momentum oscillator turns as the price simply pauses, but the trend continues. An example of this was provided in Figure 2–7.

Combining the aspect factor and the concept of momentum alleviates the problem with the simple momentum. If the market exhibits sufficient strength for the cycle to carry into a new trend, that strength can be indicated by this combination of factors, and recognition of that strength can keep you on the right side of a strongly trending market.

By multiplying the momentum, M, by the aspect factor taken over the same time period as the momentum, we get an oscillating indicator, the "market reactivity factor," ρ:

$$\rho = f \cdot M$$

where f is computed over the same period as the momentum.

For example, if you are calculating momentum for a 12-day (half-cycle) period, f is the normalized 12-day range over the total 12-day normalized volume. The 12-day reactivity is:

$$\rho_{12} = \frac{R_{12}/\overline{R}_{12}}{V_{12}/\overline{V}_{12}} (P - P_{-12})$$

where the price, P, is the midpoint price for the current interval, and P_{-12} is the 12-day ago price midpoint.

As is seen in the graphs of the reactivity indicator, the calculated data points are used along with an exponential average to provide a smoothed form of the indicator.

The 12-day range is the total range between the highest high and the lowest low of the past 12-day period. The 12-day volume is the total of the trading volume for the last 12-day period. The average 12-day range and volume, R and V, are computed as trailing exponential averages of the 12-day range and volume.

Earlier, we referred to the average period range and period volume being taken for "the recent past." If the representative recent past is too short the average values will be too erratic, and if the period is too long the averages will not be responsive enough to the changes in market conditions. Fortunately, the length of the average does not have to be precise, and extensive study has shown that using an exponential average over an equivalent period of three and a half to four complete cycle lengths works just fine. So if a 12-day indicator is used for 24-30 day cycles, then these averages are taken for about the last 100 days; that is, the smoothing constant, $\alpha = 2 / 101 = 0.02$.

It is still necessary to have a measure of how large a value of the reactivity oscillator constitutes a strongly trending market. The key to this is to use the indicator in conjunction with computed "critical ranges." A good measure of this critical range for the oscillator, either above or below zero, is given by a number that we have already calculated in the equation for the reactivity. It is the average normalized price range for the same period, R.

Research of commodity markets and of individual stocks has shown that if the reactivity indicator reaches levels beyond the average range for a given period, there is a high probability that the market will again reach the same or higher levels in the subsequent cycle. There may be just a slowing of the trend, a pause in the trend, or a reversal worthy of a trade.

The rules for the reactivity indicator (given in Chapter 3) provide a guide to simply get you out or keep you on the right side, depending on the extent by which the indicator has exceeded the critical range. In these conditions a normal momentum (and some other over-bought/over-sold indicators) would indicate a reversal of position.

The reason that the average range parameter is a good measure for the critical range is not surprising. The parameter called momentum, you will recall, is not momentum at all (in its physical definition), but a measure of the range and shape of the price curve that has occurred over the half-cycle interval. A high aspect factor multiplied times the half-cycle range will exceed the "normal" range for the interval if a strong trend is developing.

Computing a simple momentum is not sufficient; it is too narrow a measure since it only measures price action. Incorporating the volume/range relationships provides the additional measure of strength and will drive the reactivity indicator outside the critical range if there is sufficient strength to sustain the move beyond the current cycle.

A good example of this application was provided in Figures 2–7 and 2–8 on the wheat trade. With a better understanding now of why this works, go back and look at that example. Let's examine another example for the stock market. In Figure 2–21 we looked at a plot of the Dow Jones Industrial Average in the form of a range/volume chart. Using a 6-day indicator on that date to trade a roughly 15-day cycle, we get the results shown in Figure 2–22. This graph shows the 6-day reactivity and the critical ranges, and compares that with the behavior of a simple momentum.

By day 10, the reactivity had already made a significant penetration of the upper critical range, indicating that this move had more to go. The rule with the reactivity indicator is that after a penetration of the critical range you wait for the next lower peak after a crossing of zero. Even at its peak on day 12, the "momentum" turned within the range and, by itself, would have indicated a sell point.

In this case, just to remind you that trading is rarely a precise science, the behavior is a bit choppy. Between day 23 and day 37, the nominal 15-day cycle put in a double top giving you two opportunities to sell, with signals on days 27 and 34.

On Figures 2–7 and 2–22, you may have noticed that the lower critical range is not the same absolute magnitude as the upper range. Since most markets have a tendency to drop more rapidly than increase, application of the method has shown that a lower reactivity is allowed before you would hold a short position. We will always use 1.2 times the average range for the lower critical range.

More About Trading Volume

It is worth coming back to the idea of viewing the market price behavior as a function of the trading volume rather than the amount of time that has passed. Studies of some individual stocks, the narrow stock market indices, and a number of the commodities shows that there can be im-

Figure 2-22 6-Day Indicators

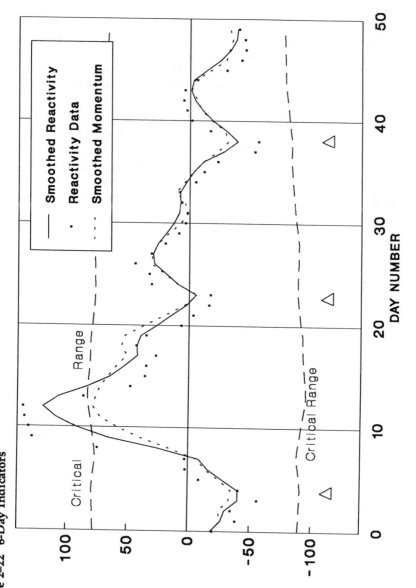

proved regularity in the cycle behavior when viewed as a function of normalized volume.

Early in the development of the reactivity indicator I had completed some studies of volume cycle behavior by examining the price cycles as a function of cumulative absolute trading volume. The dependences that I found tended to exist over a certain period of time and then change or fade away. The reason was the use of absolute volume rather than a normalized volume. Normalized volume is the ratio of the daily volume to the average daily volume.

So, each day, rather than being represented by one uniform increment of time, is represented by a quantity varying around unity, depending upon that day's volume relative to the average. A scale similar to a "day number" scale results only it is elastic; sometimes stretching out, sometimes contracting, but over the long term, remains consistent with a linear time scale.

More recent studies of the primary trading cycles used for the commodities that I trade shows that, in some cases, there is improvement in the cycle regularity in terms of this flexible scale. Or, at times, it helps to resolve why an individual cycle, say for wheat, is suddenly only 20 days instead of closer to 30. In conducting these studies, the average for the daily volume is again taken over a span of time equal to three to four times the average cycle period.

Attempting to view the markets in terms of volume instead of time has its difficulties. First of all, the market data generally comes in increments of one day; or perhaps for the Dow, increments of one hour. It does not come in increments of volume. You will recall that the procedures for detrending and for computing the indicators are all done in terms of a given number of time increments, each of which may be an entry in a spreadsheet.

The additional complexity of rigorously studying and applying the volume dependent nature of the cycles is a bit overwhelming, at least in a spreadsheet format. Since the volume dependence results in an "elastic" scale, and the cycle periods that are continually varying in the number of day intervals, the calculations for detrending and calculation of reactivity indicators become excessively complex for minimal gain.

The reactivity indicator trading system already incorporates one aspect of the volume dependence and works well in terms of a linear time scale. For some commodities, awareness of the volume effect on cycle length becomes a fine point of sophistication that can occasionally assist in a trade decision. For the sake of completeness, the trading studies in

Chapter 5 point out the cycle effects to watch for if they are a factor for that commodity.

2.7 MONITORING MONEY FLOW

The commodity market gives you information in three generally available variables: price, volume, and contract open interest. Having covered the derived variables you can get from price and from a price/volume relationship, we will now examine the open interest.

Open interest is the number of contracts that remain open at the end of each trading day. Data is generally reported as the total open interest and the net change for the day. If more traders offset (closed) positions than those that added new positions, there is a net decrease. Net changes in the number of contracts working can indicate something about the market conditions.

Discussion in the literature on the usefulness of open interest variation is usually vague, only qualitative, and not of much direct use to the short-term trader. The qualitative approach is summarized in Table 2–2. It is worth reviewing and correlating with market behavior, and it provides clues as to whether a price move is a new trend or just a position-covering move.

A better approach, which complements the reactivity indicator, is an indicator developed by John Herrick of Herrick Investor Tutoring. It combines price change, volume, and open interest change in a mathematical attempt to measure the flow of money into, or out of, a given market.

The basic measure of money flow, MF, is:

$$MF = C \cdot V(M - M_y)\left(1 \pm \frac{2|\Delta|}{I}\right)$$

where: C = dollar value of 1-point move
V = trading volume
M = daily mean price, subscript y indicating yesterday's
Δ = change in open interest
I = the larger of today's or yesterday's open interest

The | | around the delta indicates absolute value; i.e., always positive whether the change in open interest is up or down. The + or - in the last term is + if the mean price, M, has gone up or - if the price has gone down.

Table 2–2   Qualitative View of Changes in Open Interest

OPEN INTEREST	PRICES	EXPECTATIONS
↑	↑	higher prices
↑	→	trading range
↑	↓	lower prices
↓	↑	short covering rally —watch for top
↓	→	trading range
↓	↓	beginning of downtrend
→	any direction	indecisive

In this form, this *MF* parameter is a large number and very erratic. Once again, to tame the variation, we use an exponential average.

I don't know how John Herrick applied this index. Thomas Aspray[3] used weekly data and then looked for values above and below zero, divergences with price, breaking of trendlines, crossing of moving averages, etc., possibly somewhat beyond its actual potential.

The interest here is in a supplemental index to use with the reactivity indicator, so our demands on this indicator will be more reasonable. The most useful application is the "divergence" of the *MF* with price. A divergence occurs when a subsequent top or bottom in the indicator is of lower magnitude, while the corresponding top or bottom in price is larger. Then

---

3   *Payoff Index, Technical Analysis of Stocks and Commodities*, March, 1988.

a line drawn across the peaks would in one case slant upward, and in the other case, downward.

The more important price trend changes are generally preceded by a change in trend in MF. This is most easily identified by maintaining a plot of midpoint price and MF, and noting divergences at tops or bottoms. Such a divergence, coupled with a trade indication from the reactivity indicator, gives a high probability of a successful trade.

To get the value of MF to be in about the same range as the price range, it is divided by a scaling factor, K. In the smoothed adjusted form, we have:

$$MF^s = \frac{MF^s_y + \alpha(MF - MF^s_y)}{K}$$

The superscript, s, is used to denote the smoothed value which is the only form we will use and so we will revert to just calling it MF.

The typical smoothing constant, α, is 0.1 and the scaling factor, K, is about 100,000. Although the dollar value per point has a given value, for our purpose it can be combined with the scaling factor and a value selected to give a suitable range. Since MF is an oscillator which varies around zero, we can make it vary around an "artificial zero" at a convenient level to plot on the same graph as the price midpoint by adding an average of the midpoint price to the index.

Figure 2–23 shows the daily midpoint price and the MF for cotton during a portion of 1988. There are two clear divergent patterns which showed excellent trade potential. Using a 6-day and an 18-day reactivity, a sell signal was given on day 119 and a buy signal on day 165. The corresponding MF-price divergence that formed by these days signaled a high reliability trade.

The behavior of the MF is different for different commodities and some time should be spent studying the historical patterns. One of the main differences is the time between the trend change in the MF and the price trend change.

The time between the divergent peaks is indicative of the period of the cycle that is turning. For example, a divergence of 5 to 10 days may indicate a 30-day cycle turning point, whereas a divergence that takes 30 days to develop indicates a major longer term cycle turning point.

In the case of Eurodollars (Figure 2–24) the divergence that is most common is usually 8-12 days and corresponds to the short-term timing cycle and occurs with the turn in the 25- to 35-day cycle. For copper, if there is a divergence, it's usually short—about five to eight days.

Figure 2-23   Daily Midpoint and Money Flow

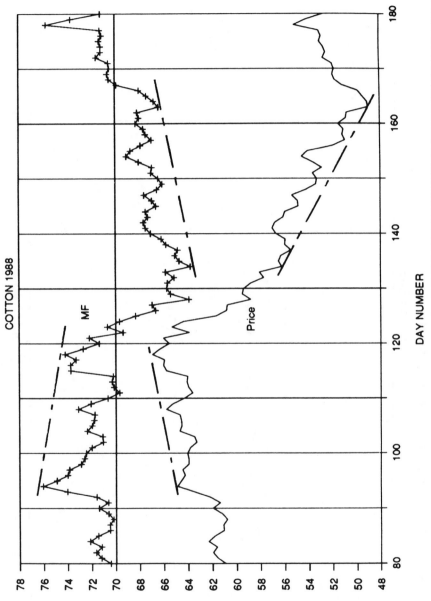

Figure 2-24 Midpoint and Money Flow—Eurodollars

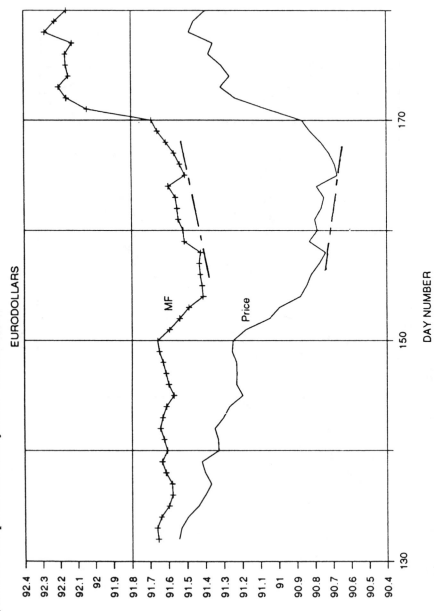

This is a supporting indicator used in conjunction with the reactivity. A price-*MF* divergence is not a requirement for a trade. Many good trades, as indicated by the reactivity indicators, are not accompanied by such a divergence.

It is interesting to note that when the index is predominantly above zero (money flowing in) or below zero (money flowing out) during periods of trading range price behavior, it indicates accumulation or distribution and can hint at breakout direction.

2.8 ADDITIONAL INDICATORS FOR STOCK INDEX FUTURES

All the concepts previously discussed apply equally well to trading stock index futures as to the other commodity futures. The stock market is, however, basically different from other markets in the amount of readily available information. There are a number of other technical indicators that have been developed to use this information. Those that I have found as useful supplemental indicators are presented here. The type of information is different because it is information on the cash market, not the futures market.

Cash vs Futures

In addition to the price, volume and open interest of the index futures, there is ready access to price and volume of the cash market and a host of other variables that are commonly grouped as "market internals." These include issues advancing, issues declining, advancing volume, declining volume, number of block trades, new highs, and new lows. If you don't have on-line quote services or obtain the numbers off a cable TV station's ticker, you can get hourly data on the Dow Industrials in *The Wall Street Journal* or *Investor's Daily*.

The old saying, "Cash is King," is certainly operative in the futures markets, particularly in the financial markets. The difference between the futures and the cash price is called the "premium." This relationship between futures and cash is relatively fixed according to the time remaining on the maturity of the futures contract—a carrying charge, that gets smaller as you approach the delivery month.

The practice of trading on the variation in the premium is called index arbitrage trading, or simply "program trading," and despite considerable controversy, is done in large volume on the S&P 500 and the Major Market Indices. This practice adds considerable short-term volatility which can be annoying to the trader. It does, however, assure that the spread between futures and cash prices never gets very far from theoretical.

In trading futures and options on stock indices, the use of the cash price is advantageous because of the readily available data. The major indices on the New York Stock Exchange which are represented on the futures or options exchanges (S&P 100, S&P 500, NYSE Composite and the Major Market Index) are well represented by the Dow Jones Industrial Average. This means that you can use the readily available data, including the hourly data on the Dow Jones Index to trade index options and futures.

Using Market Internals

Probably the most widely used data beyond price and volume in the stock market is the number of issues advancing and number of issues declining. The usual way of presenting this is the advance/decline ratio, or A/D ratio. Other derivative indicators covered here that use the advance, decline data include one that I call the "Issues Index," and an over-bought, over-sold indicator using a 30-day cumulative A/D ratio.

Hand in hand with the advancing and declining issues is the trading volume of the advancing and declining issues. These volumes are combined with the number of advancing and declining issues to create the short-term trading index, TRIN, or also known as the "Arms" index after Richard Arms who first popularized this indicator.

The Issues Index

One of the most useful ways in which to use the number of advancing and declining issues is to express the net number of advancers or decliners as a percentage of total issues traded:

$$N = 100 \cdot \frac{A - D}{A + D + U}$$

The denominator is total issues traded; that is, advances, declines and unchanged. This parameter is erratic and is tamed by taking a 12-day running exponential average (0.15 smoothing constant) to obtain the issues index, I:

$$I = I_y + 0.15 \cdot (N - I_y)$$

where I_y is yesterday's index.

A most useful feature of this parameter is as an early indication of sentiment change. This is shown by the divergence between the issues index and price. Figures 2–25 and 2–26 show the issues index and the S&P 500 futures for a portion of 1988. You can see a number of divergent points as indicated at almost all the major short-term tops and bottoms. Each of these points provided excellent trade points.

Divergences which occur when the issues index exceeds + or - 10 are highly reliable trade indications. Divergences in the intermediate range between +10 and -10 are sometimes good and sometimes not. This emphasizes that the issues index is used as a secondary indicator in conjunction with the reactivity indicators. It provides good verification of trade points.

Two Good Over-bought/Over-sold Indicators

All sorts of oscillators are used to describe the stock market as being "over-bought" or "over-sold." Many times, you will hear one analyst say the market is over-bought, while another says it is over-sold. So what do these expressions mean? All they are trying to do is to measure extremes in market sentiment; the implication being that price has moved past value and therefore should reverse in order to correct itself.

Sometimes opinions differ because they are referring to different time frames, and sometimes they are meaningless. Using extreme values in price stochastics or momentums, for example, can be wrong because extreme readings mean the market is very strong (or weak) and is going to continue that trend. Describing a market as over-bought, OB, or over-sold, OS, also requires that the time frame be specified because obviously the market can get over-bought on a short-term basis while near a long-term over-sold condition.

A good longer-term (50-100 day) OB-OS indicator is the 30-day summation A/D ratio:

$$OB/OS = \frac{Total\ daily\ advances}{Total\ daily\ declines}$$

or adding the last 30 days of the number of advancing issues and dividing by the sum of the last 30 days of the number of declining issues.

This oscillator (Figure 2–27) varies around 1.0 and indicates OB condition if it goes above 1.2 and oversold if it gets below 0.84. It is also a good indicator of trend. As it declines approaching 1.0 and goes negative

Figure 2–25 Issues Index

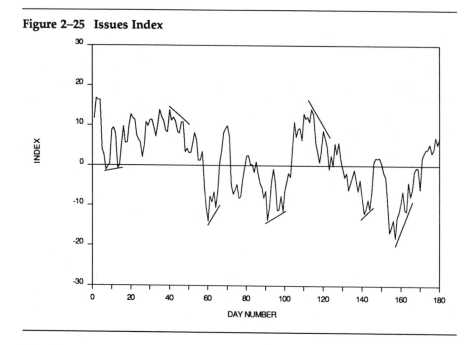

Figure 2–26 S&P 500 Index

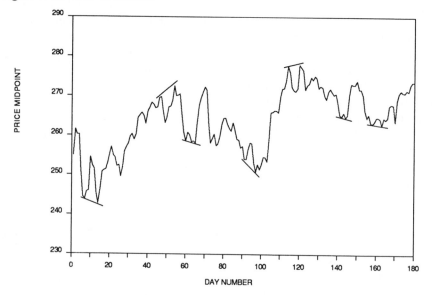

Figure 2–27   30-Day Cumulative A/D, OB/OS Ratio

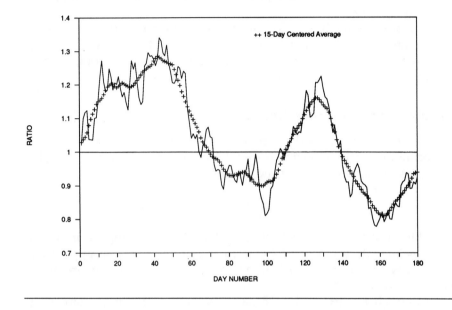

Figure 2–28   NYSE Composite Index

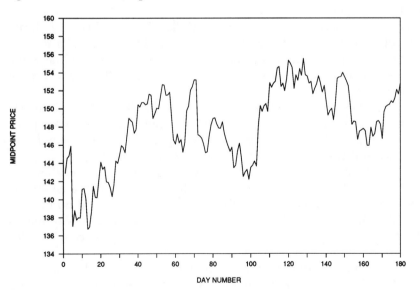

the trend is down and as it rises approaching 1.0 and into positive terri-
tory the trend is up. Compare Figure 2-27 and the NYSE Composite Index
shown in Figure 2–28.

A shorter-term OB/OS indicator is the issues index presented above.
In addition to its value as an indicator of tops and bottoms by its divergence with price, it indicates the market is short-term over-bought when
the indicator exceeds 10, or over-sold when less than -10.

Plurality and the Advance-Decline Line

The plurality index, p, is the running total of the net number of issues
advancing or declining, which is calculated each day as yesterday's plurality plus the advances minus the declines:

$$p = p_y + (A - D)$$

This basic concept, first applied by Paul Dysart, is applied in different forms to make it more well-behaved and useful. The basic application
is generally the same, i.e., a leading (or divergent) indicator presaging
sentiment change.

Although Dysart used a 15-day summation, the more commonly
used form is the continuing summation given above and is often called
the advance-decline line, or AD line. It is a measure of the "breadth" of
market participation.

The most useful attribute of the AD line is its ability to indicate
intermediate term trend change by virtue of a divergence in its tops or
bottoms with tops or bottoms in price. Lower tops in the AD line while
the market makes higher tops indicates a lack of breadth and a turning
point in prices.

Such a case is illustrated in Figures 2–29 and 2–30. Looking at the AD
line you see a top at X and a lower top at Y. Meanwhile, the market price
shows the top at Y to be higher than the top at X. This is a significant
divergence and was followed by a significant market decline.

A useful adjunct to the AD line is the use of the commonly available
advancing and declining volume data. It is formulated in the same way as
the AD line except that you use the volume instead of the number of
issues. This indicator is also shown on Figure 2–29. The Av-Dv line is
useful for indicating shorter term turning points by divergence with price
as shown.

It is also an indicator of longer term market strength and the accumulation of stocks. The continuing higher bottoms of the Av-Dv line (Figure

Figure 2–29   Cumulative A&D and Av-Dv

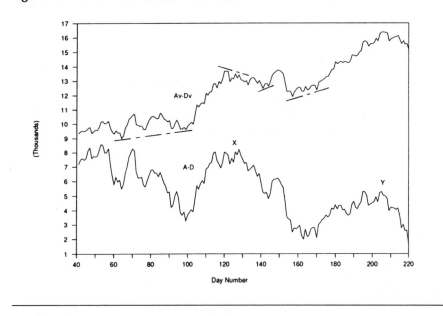

Figure 2–30   Dow Jones Industrials

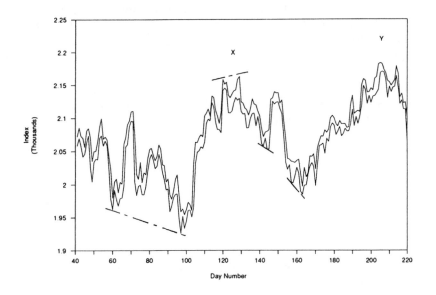

2–29) foretold a later strong rally in stocks. A presentation of the use of the advancing and declining volume, although somewhat idealized, is provided by Lander.[4]

The Arms Index (TRIN)

A popular short-term index indicator of the market sentiment is the Arms index (developed by Richard Arms), commonly referred to as the TRIN. This indicator is computed as a combination of the advancing and declining issues and the corresponding advancing and declining volume.

$$TRIN = \frac{A/D}{V_a/V_d}$$

It is a ratio of ratios and indicates a concentration of volume in the advancing or declining stocks, indicating bullish or bearish sentiment, respectively.

The TRIN is best used as an indicator of intra-day strength. A value of 1.0 is neutral with lower values bullish and higher values bearish. Values of about 0.75 or less indicate strength, and values over about 1.2 indicate weakness. A value of about 0.5 or less after the first hour of trading gives a high probability of a strong continuing rally for that day.

It is also frequently used as a 10-day trailing average for indication of market sentiment. When the 10-day average value gets to 0.8 or below, it indicates "over-bought" conditions and one can expect a sell-off. Usually the sell-off doesn't get underway until the 10-day TRIN works its way back up to around 0.9 or 1.0. Similarly, values of 1.2 or greater indicate an "over-sold" condition.

Perhaps a good sentiment indicator, my experience has shown that this trailing average form is not useful for trading. This can be verified by comparing Figures 2–31 and 2–30.

---

4   John Lander, "Cumulative Volume and Momentum," *Stocks and Commodities,* January and February, 1988.

Figure 2–31 10-Day Trailing Average TRIN

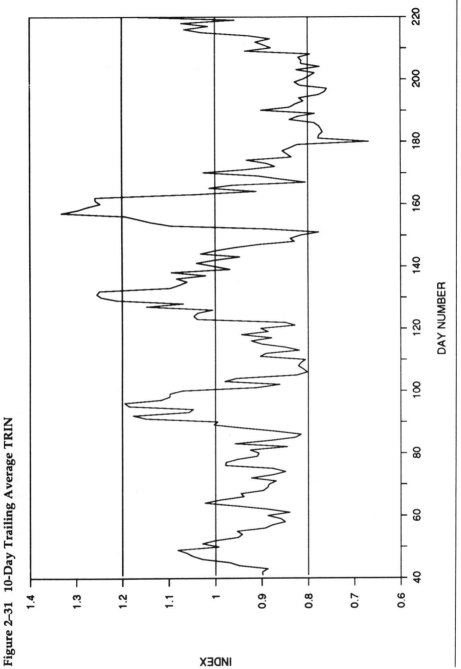

3

The Application

■ ■ ■

The test of a vocation is the love of the drudgery it involves.

Logan Pearsall Smith

It is in the application of the technical concepts that the actual, sometimes tedious work begins. Hopefully you got involved in all this with the understanding that there is still no such thing as easy money. But like any other profession, getting started is the toughest part. Later, as you are reaping the benefits of this work, and enjoying the short hours and independence, you can look back and see that it was worth it.

With the technical foundations now in place, this chapter discusses selecting some commodities to trade, getting data, and setting up the computer spreadsheets in preparation for trading.

Most of the work described in this chapter can be bypassed by purchasing the spreadsheet templates referred to on the mail-in form included at the back of this book. Each template includes recent data, programming of all the necessary equations, and setup of the graphic displays. The templates are available for nine different commodities and are programmed with the then current cycle lengths appropriate to each commodity. Even if you are fluent in spreadsheet use, considerable time can be saved by using one template as a reference in creating your own for other commodities.

3.1 WHAT MARKETS TO TRADE

Any of the actively traded markets can be considered for trading. You may have a particular interest in a given stock or commodity because of some current or past business involvement, or perhaps you like the sound of pork bellies or soybeans. But there are a few things about a market that you should consider before you elect to trade it. Some you can tell by looking at the price charts; some take more in-depth study.

Market Character

Some successful traders say that it is important to keep your trading system "simple." Simple is a relative term. My system may seem simple to me, but complex to Williams,[1] who stresses simplicity. But, like systems, the simpler markets usually trade better by market timing systems than complex markets.

The simplest markets are those that are a basic product rather than a by-product; the producers are a relatively homogeneous group, the consumers are a homogeneous group, and it's best if producers and consumers are in the same culture and/or country. Few, if any, markets meet these criteria, but some are closer than others.

Consider the live hog market, for example. The producers are primarily in the Midwestern farming areas, and the consumers are primarily in the United States. Both producers and consumers are subject to the same cultural pressures, beliefs, diets, etc. Also important, they use the same currency. This is a primary product (as opposed to the pork bellies which is a by-product market). The traders in the market are a relatively homogeneous group; that is, the producers, processors and speculators are primarily in the United States.

These factors resulted in a market behavior that has been cyclically well behaved. And, for a trading method which identifies and uses cycles,

---

1   Larry Williams, *Definitive Guide to Futures Trading*, Windsor Books, Brightwaters, NY, 1988.

that's exactly what we like to see. The seasonal tendencies have been reasonably regular, and the shorter term cycles, which are primarily the result of sentiment shifts, have been also regular.

Within a homogeneous cultural group, or interest group, the ebb and flow of sentiment is fairly regular. The combination of seasons, the gestation period of hogs, the market reception of pork products, and the trader's sentiments have all reacted in concert to produce a lovely harmony into which you can tune to make money as a speculator.

The financial markets are typically not as regular. The bond market, for example, was originally a good market to trade by cycle methods. It was as close to a "source" product as you could get in the financial markets. And, as with most other markets, was a domestic market. Even the government's influence on that market is subject to common cultural tendencies.

Now a sizeable portion of the bond market is in the hands of foreigners. To some extent, those cultural differences influence the cyclical tendencies. It is further complicated by currency exchange rates, worldwide banking policy, etc. And now that they have instituted a night session, it is a matter of preference if, after a day of market monitoring, you want to spend your evenings at it as well.

Most markets are now, in fact, international markets to varying degrees. This has added complexity to the cyclical structure of the price behavior. However, the use of cycles to describe the behavior is still a most effective trading tool. You just have to allow some flexibility, and to re-examine the cyclical structure every year or so to see if things may have changed.

The cotton market cycles did an abrupt change in July of 1985 when a new international contract was instituted. But the market is just marching to a different beat now and is still tradable in a cyclical manner. Each market has its own character, and the cotton market has its own special tricks to surprise the unwary trader.

The stock market is certainly a by-product market whose character has changed considerably in the 1980s. The ebb and flow of sentiment is still there, but many complicating factors have been superimposed. These include the widespread use of computer-generated trading systems used in futures to cash arbitrage, futures hedging strategies for portfolio insurance, speculating systems, as well as the growing influence of international monetary policies, and international trading. Nevertheless, the reactivity indications allow good profit-making trades and, of course, futures trading has never been a tame game.

These generalities aside, market "character" can also be somewhat cyclical. Any given market may show consistent behavior for a time, perhaps measured in years, and at other times show greater variation in cycle parameters.

Cycle Character

The character of the market is reflected in the cyclical behavior it exhibits. When evaluating a commodity to trade by cyclically based methods, there are two basic cycle characteristics to evaluate. These are the cycle regularity and the cycle amplitude, or range.

Regularity

Cycle regularity is the consistency of the cycle length. This can best be measured by the standard deviation found in a statistically significant number of cycles. To be traded reliably, the standard deviation, after discarding the highest and lowest value, should be less than about 20 percent of the average cycle period.

For example, detrend some commodity over 25 cycle lengths. Discard the longest and shortest period to eliminate the occasional cycle jump. Then calculate the standard deviation and determine if it is less than about 20 percent of the cycle length. If you don't have the means to determine standard deviation, just find the average cycle length and determine if about eight out of ten cycle lengths are within 20 percent of the average. Cycles, with length variations greater than these guidelines, can be difficult to trade.

Cycle Range

Besides finding the cycles of adequate consistency (almost every market has one or more), it is necessary to trade a cycle of adequate range to achieve a reasonable payoff. You can think of this in terms of risk vs reward. There is a degree of uncertainty in the entry and exit points; therefore, you want the potential reward to be many times that uncertainty.

After detrending the price data as discussed further in the next section, examine the average price range of the cycle you're considering for short-term trading. Generally, a short-term cycle should have an average cycle range of at least 3.5 times the average daily range.

An equivalent 30-day exponential average ($\alpha = 0.065$) of the daily range is a good measure for average daily range. The average cycle range should be taken over the last four to six cycles.

Trading Volume

It is best to avoid thinly traded markets. Thin markets are those that have average daily trading volume of less than about 3,000 to 4,000 contracts (all months). Although the market behavior can still be represented by the reactivity indicator, you can get bad fills. Thinly traded markets are subject to greater short-term volatility because the price is easily moved by the larger trades of commercial interests. This, and the apparent leeway on where the floor-trader makes your trade (particularly if he/she is trading his own account) can result in some surprising fills, usually bad. Your fill may be far from where the market was last quoted. Also, the ease with which the price can be moved can result in the hitting of a few stop-loss orders, which can then drive the market quickly through a lot of stops.

When considering whether or not the market you're trading is thin, you must consider the particular contract you're trading. If you don't follow the individual contract volume, you should try to be trading the contract with the largest open interest since that is where most of the trading volume is likely to be.

3.2 DETRENDING

Having selected the markets you wish to trade, you must gather historical data. This will be used for detrending analysis and practice trading of the cycle you choose to trade. There are sources for most of the data that you are likely to need from which you can download the data from a database via your modem, or you can purchase it on floppy disc. A good reference for these services is the *Microcomputer Resource Guide*, published annually by the American Association of Individual Investors in Chicago.

Again, the order card in the back of the book gives a listing of data available from the author on disc at nominal cost.

Analyzing historical data is just naturally boring to some. However, it's worth noting again that all we will ever deal with in technical analysis is historical data. The history may be as recent as a few minutes, but it is history. We are going to base our expectations on history repeating in some approximate fashion. We are not in the business of foretelling the future.

It is necessary to study more than just the recent past to determine the approximate repetitive cycles which are exhibited in the given commodity to be studied and traded. Much of this analysis has been done previously by others; however, cyclical patterns can change over time. Part of an effective trading strategy is to always carry along a detrending array to help in defining where you are in each cycle when considering a trade. It is important to have a good understanding of the detrending technique, as well as having established the detrending analysis for future use.

Even for relatively short-term trading, it can be important to know where you are in the longer-term cycles. These are of secondary or supporting interest to the short-term trader, but the longer term cycles are defining the trend within which you are trading. They can also tell you when to anticipate a change in trend and aid in determining when to hang on to a position and add to it at the turns in the shorter cycles. Many commodities exhibit semi-annual or annual (usually referred to as seasonal), and longer cycles. The study of these cycles is best done with weekly data. I recommend a minimum of five to ten years of weekly data and two to three years of daily data.

For weekly data, we are only using one number per week—the weekly midpoint, so seven years of data is only about 350 numbers. If we are looking for cycles of a roughly one-year duration, this will give us only seven cycles. This is not a statistically large number; however, since the character of the markets can change over many years, longer term data is not always useful because a dominant cycle length may change. Since we are typically looking to trade cycles of somewhere between 25 to 50 days duration (6 to 12 weeks), and since we are going to continuously update the detrending analysis, longer term data is not essential.

Cycles of less than about 15 weeks need daily data to sufficiently reduce scatter, and for short-term trading cycles (less than about 10–12 days) consider using hourly data. Given the cycle lengths of interest and the need for at least 15 cycle periods, we need at least 3 years (759 trading days) of daily data.

For detrending purposes, we are only going to use the midpoint of each day's range. However, the data should be gathered in the same format as you will use for your daily updating; that is, high, low, close, trading volume, and change in open interest. This daily data will also be your practice trading data.

The detrending analysis, presented in Chapter 2, can be summarized as follows:

1. Display the data array graphically. Use a sufficiently expanded time scale to see the cycles you are looking for (break into several graphs if necessary). The shorter cycles will be analyzed first to average these out as we proceed to the longer cycles.

2. Take a running centered average over the length that you have chosen and subtract it from the data. It is usually helpful to subtract the first cycle from a three-interval average of the data, rather than the raw data, to eliminate some scatter. Graphically display the result.

3. Examine again the cycle bottoms and see if the cycle you wanted is there. Tabulate the distances between the bottoms and find the average period. If the average period differs from what you used for the running average, you may wish to do another iteration using the new period.

4. Examining the results of the first detrend will help you find other cycles; for example, a 20-week detrend may indicate a 10-week cycle, and may show more important bottoms at 40-week intervals indicating a 40-week cycle.

5. Continue the analysis by subtracting the longer period cycle averages from the shorter period averages to get the lengths and the approximate amplitudes of each cycle.

Using standard spreadsheet software for these analyses, it is convenient to enter the data into the spreadsheet in columns. Put headings in the first row so you will know what is in each column. Number the data in the first column, place the high in the second column, the low in the next, and so on.

You must get familiar with the "copy" command as you will want to copy formulas down a column to get the analytical results. For numbering you simply enter "1" into the first cell under the heading; for example, cell A2, and enter the formula A2+1 in the next row. Then, use the copy command and copy that little formula to all the cells in the column as far down as the number of data points you have and, presto, your data is numbered. You may then wish to replace formulas with values to eliminate the formulas and leave the numbers to conserve memory space.

Similarly, in another column, enter the formula for calculating the midpoint; then in the next column, calculate the first average, and in the next, subtract the average from the midpoint. This is your first "detrend." Remember that you are using a centered average so the cell containing the formula for the average should be at a position in the column at the midpoint of the range over which the average is taken. Then, when you graphically display the data, the data points will be in the right place.

For the next longer term cycle, you will subtract an average over the range of the period you are looking for from the average over the shorter

Table 3–1   Copper Detrend Array

A Day #	B High	C Low	D Mid	E 3-Day Avg	F 9-Day Avg	G 9-Day Dtrnd	H 32-Day Avg	I 32-Day Dtrnd
16	104.9	102.0	103.4	104.2	102.8	1.4	103.3	−0.5
17	105.8	103.5	104.6	103.8	103.1	0.7	103.9	−0.8
18	104.1	103.0	103.5	108.8	103.6	0.2	104.5	−0.9
19	103.6	103.0	103.3	103.1	104.2	−1.1	105.1	−0.9
20	103.4	102.0	102.7	103.2	104.8	−1.6	105.6	−0.8
21	104.7	103.0	103.8	103.7	105.8	−2.1	106.2	−0.4
22	105.5	103.9	104.7	105.2	106.5	−1.3	106.7	−0.2
23	109.0	105.5	107.2	107.4	107.4	0.0	107.2	0.2
24	112.2	108.8	110.5	109.8	108.4	1.4	107.5	0.9
25	112.8	110.6	111.7	111.2	109.2	2.0	107.9	1.3
26	112.3	110.6	111.4	111.5	109.8	1.7	108.3	1.5
27	111.8	110.8	111.3	111.6	110.6	1.0	108.7	1.9
28	113.3	110.9	112.1	111.1	111.4	−0.3	109.1	2.3
29	111.5	108.5	110.0	110.5	111.8	−1.3	109.5	2.3
30	111.3	108.0	109.6	110.5	112.0	−1.5	109.8	2.2
31	114.2	109.5	111.8	111.8	112.1	−0.3	110.1	2.0
32	115.1	113.0	114.0	113.4	112.4	1.0	110.4	2.0
33	115.5	113.4	114.4	114.0	112.5	1.5	110.7	1.8
34	114.6	112.5	113.5	113.5	112.7	0.8	110.9	1.8
35	113.5	111.6	112.5	113.4	112.6	0.8	111.2	1.4
36	115.8	112.4	114.1	113.2	112.3	0.9	111.5	0.8
37	114.5	111.8	113.1	112.7	111.7	1.0	111.7	0.0
38	112.1	110.1	111.1	111.1	111.4	−0.3	111.8	−0.4

cycle which you have already taken. In this way, you isolate each cycle and get a measure of the amplitude of each cycle component.

An example of such a detrending array is shown in Table 3-1 for copper. The nine-day detrend (column G) is obtained by subtracting column F from column E. Similarly, the 32-day detrend is obtained by subtracting H from F. This table is extracted from a spreadsheet which begins at day 1; however since the averages are centered averages, the first 32-day average is taken at day 16 and includes the midpoint data from day 1 through day 31.

Spreadsheet users may have other favorite ways of arranging data for this type of calculation. This example is convenient and compatible with the functions and graphical options of Lotus 1-2-3, version 2.1. This data can conveniently be viewed graphically by using an x-y plot specifying column A for the x-range and columns G and I as data ranges. Refer to Figures 2-16, 2-17, 2-18 and 2-19 for examples of graphs of data detrends.

3.3 SETTING UP THE TRADING ARRAY

The trading array, or spreadsheet, contains the raw data, equations, and the computed results that are used on a daily basis to make trading decisions. The contents of the spreadsheet can be divided into six basic groups:

> The input data
> Computed stop-loss points
> The reactivity computation
> The money flow computation
> The running cycle detrend
> Computed weekly midpoint data (optional)

The spreadsheet array for the typical commodity has about 40 columns. It is generally useful to maintain the data for the last 120 to 140 days in the trading spreadsheet. The input data can be periodically stored separately for possible future study purposes and the calculated data older than 140 days discarded. This keeps the spreadsheet at a workable size.

Input Data

The input data used for commodity futures trading consists of the price high, low and close, the trading volume and the change in the open interest. For an individual stock, there will be no open interest data. The price close is for reference only in this system since each day is represented by the midpoint between the high and low. Some technicians advocate giving weight to the close by averaging the high, low and close as the "midpoint." It's your choice.

You will also want a column for day numbers and one for the date. The date is only for reference. I find just entering Fridays keeps things oriented, and I use it to cue the computation of the weekly midpoint.

This is a good start at establishing the spreadsheet with the first seven columns; day number, date, high, low, close, volume, and change in open interest. This is all of the input data and these are the independent variables. Most of the time, this is the only portion of the spreadsheet that you will view. The other parameters of interest will be viewed in graphical form.

The rest of the spreadsheet consists of dependent variables in that they are computed using one or more of the input data. Therefore, the rest of the spreadsheet at the current day will have equations in the cells.

Computed Stop-Loss Points

The next group will be the calculated parameters that go into determining the stop-loss points using the equations presented in section 4.3. I keep these in the columns next to the input data because, although I display the stop-loss data on the price graph, I want to look at the specific numbers. Having them in or near the normally viewed part of the spreadsheet eliminates the need to move around the spreadsheet.

To keep the cell equations from becoming too cumbersome, the computations are broken into convenient smaller pieces. Also, these individual pieces may be used in other computations, so it is better to keep them separate. It is sometimes helpful to examine some of the separate pieces just to be better informed of what is occurring, and to make sure everything looks right. It is not impossible for errors to creep in, especially if you are doing some changes to the spreadsheet. I break this computation into seven columns:

The price midpoint
The smoothed extrapolated midpoint
The daily range

The average daily range
The standard deviation of daily range
The long stop-point
The short stop-point

Since these columns can be in any order, moving the last two to the left keeps them in easy view.

The Reactivities

Here, we use the equations developed in Section 2.6. This is the heart of the trading system. The number of columns allotted depends on the number of cycles you choose to track with these indicators. For each cycle length, you will need:

The average volume
The half-cycle price range
The average range
The negative average range
The reactivity
The smoothed reactivity

Normally, just two reactivity indicators will be used: one for the primary cycle and one for the short cycle. For other cycles that I may wish to follow, I use simple momentums. Include a column for a negative of the average range to show + and − critical ranges on the reactivity graph. Reactivity indicators for two cycle lengths require 12 columns.

The smoothing constant used in the exponential average for the reactivity depends upon the period being used for the reactivity calculation. For tracking the short-term trading cycle (4- to 8-day reactivity) a smoothing factor of about 0.4 gives good response. For a 12- to 15-day reactivity, use 0.33, and use 0.2 for anything longer. The importance of the smoothed line is that it provides a reference to screen out the small irregularities in the actual data points. In the case of the short-cycle indicator, the trade signal is given by the data point crossing the smoothed line.

Money Flow

The modified Herrick index applied to daily data, which I call "money flow," is presented in Section 2.7. In establishing the equations in the spreadsheet, I first compute the last term on the right, the fractional open interest change, using the ABS function for the change in the open interest. It is easier to then compute the rest of the equation using a conditional statement on the price change to select the use of the plus or minus sign within the bracketed term.

Since the money flow indicator is used in conjunction with the price midpoint, it is convenient to use a "translated" value which can be put on the same graph as the price midpoint. It is then easy to spot the development of divergences between the price and money flow. This can be accomplished by adding to the equation for the MF, a constant which roughly represents a median value of price over the period displayed on the graph. The median value is the translated zero line for the MF indicator and should be included on the graph for reference.

Having calculated the basic MF, use a separate column that computes the exponentially smoothed result, which is the value that actually gets used. We then have five columns for the MF computation:

The open interest
The fractional change
The raw normalized MF
The smoothed MF
The translated zero line value

The associated graph plots the price midpoint, the smoothed MF and the translated zero line.

The Running Detrend

In the spreadsheet for each commodity, it is useful to carry along a running detrend of the most important cycles, particularly the primary and trading cycles. This allows a quick graphical reference to see where the last top or bottom was as reference for where the trading window is expected. Keeping track of the cycle periods also can tell you if there is a tendency for the cycle length to be undergoing some shift.

This detrend array looks just like that described earlier in Section 3.2, Table 3-1. In the detrending studies we looked at a lot of history whereas in the trading array we just carry the last 120 to 140 days, the same as for the rest of the trading indicators.

The speed and memory capacity of your computer may be a consideration here. The detrend information is not something that you need to look at every day so it can be kept in a separate spreadsheet. However, it is useful to show the detrend of a cycle on the same graph as the reactivity indicator which is tracking it, and the centered average data can be used for the past data in the reactivity calculation. For example, a 12-day indicator tracking an approximate 30-day cycle would use the short cycle average for the 12-day-ago data.

Weekly Midpoint Data

Keeping track of the weekly data is not a direct part of the trading system, and you may wish to ignore it. Maybe you would just find it a distraction. But in the interest of knowing as much as possible about what is occurring, and what has been occurring, keeping the weekly midpoint data lets you know where things are in the seasonal cycles and in the long-term cycles. It also allows occasionally looking back over several years to see what the historic highs and lows have been.

This data is primarily for reference purposes. Occasionally, it has direct bearing on your trading decision. The seasonal tendencies can certainly affect the strength of your trade, but for short-term trading, they are not reliable. The daily trading indicators tell you what to do. Perhaps the weekly data can tell you the best time to be out of the market and go on vacation.

You need a column in which you compute the weekly midpoint (or two columns for the weekly high and low if you prefer), a column for week numbers, and a column for the weekly data. The computing column is part of the daily data array and is a conditional statement which computes a number only on the last day of the week. I key off the date column which I only enter each Friday. If there is a value entered in the date column, it uses the MAX and MIN functions to find the highest and lowest of the daily data and computes the midpoint.

I carry the weekly data at the extreme right of my spreadsheet and keep the column lengths about the same as the daily data so I always have 120 to 140 weeks of data to view graphically if I like. I periodically transfer this to a weekly spreadsheet for each commodity where I do some weekly cycle studies.

Spreadsheet Maintenance

During the development of the computer methods, and in my early use of these methods, I used a PC with 640k RAM and no hard disc. I occasionally ran out of memory in doing long-term detrending or trading studies, and these occurrences prompted me to utilize whatever means at my disposal to minimize storage requirements. But the most critical problem, when trading a half dozen or more different commodities and stocks, each with its own spreadsheet, was the time required to read and write the spreadsheet file.

With a 486-based machine and a low-access-time hard disc the array size described above is very fast. Still there is data management to do. The most important things to do to maintain speed and efficiency are:

1. Keep the data array to the minimum workable size. For me, carrying the past 120 to 140 days as described above is about right. You can separate the detrend portion and the weekly data to another spreadsheet if you find things are too slow.

2. Periodically, use a Range Value function to replace equations in the cells with their computed values.

Since we are adding a row of data each day, the spreadsheet is constantly growing, so obviously we must periodically do some maintenance to keep it down to size and efficient. There are four steps to do each 10 or 20 days as follows:

1. Change the x-range and the data ranges of the graphs as necessary. A convenient way to set up the graphs is to maintain the ranges to a point beyond 120 to 140 day array, say to 200, and change the beginning (left) end of the range to view the portion that you want.

2. Move the entire array up 10 or 20 days. If you are saving historical data, be sure you have saved the raw data in the part you are moving off the array, or it will be lost. Also, if you are viewing the entire range in the spreadsheet in any of the graphs, the range must be changed before you move the array up to keep it within the data array.

3. Copy all the equation columns down another 10 or 20 days. This is done quickly and easily with the Copy commands.

4. Replace formulas with values where things have already been computed to eliminate equations, thereby reducing the calculation time and saving memory.

When you get proficient at these operations, it only takes a few minutes for each spreadsheet, and you only need to do them once every 10 or 20 days as you choose. All of these steps can be automated using MACRO routines in your spreadsheet software. But most importantly, DON'T FORGET TO SAVE THE SPREADSHEET after you have done the maintenance work.

Trade Records

It is obviously important to keep accurate and organized records of trades made. These need to be on two levels; one which is a daily worksheet on which you enter trades as you make them, noting contract, quantity, price, date, perhaps an order number, whether the position is open or closed, and the values for stop-loss points. The other is a more permanent record—more of an accounting record, keeping track of all closed trades, net profits, year to date, account balance, and so on.

You never want a trade operating that you don't remember, and you want to be able to see at a glance what your open trades are at any time. When you open your account, the brokerage firm will give you a booklet of some kind in which to record your trades. You may find it more effective to use a format that you establish for yourself.

Contract Change-over

Generally, the contract month that we will be trading is the one in which there is the highest open interest. The assumption is that most of the trading volume will be in that contract, thereby providing the most liquidity. You will want to change to a later contract month as the open interest changes, or as you approach the First Notice Date.

If there is no price discrepancy between contracts, you could simply start entering the data from the new contract into the spreadsheet. However, there is almost always sufficient difference to affect the indicators, and sometimes the differences are quite large. It is not unusual, for example, to see differences of four or five cents a pound between the August and the October hog contracts, or perhaps more than ten cents per bushel between contracts in wheat.

The simplest approach is to retrieve from your data service the historical price data for the past 60 to 100 days for the new contract that you wish to trade. Copy this price data into the spreadsheet and then copy all the equations back as many rows as necessary to calculate the indicators with the new data. Then "Range Value" these rows again to reduce the number of cells carrying equations to maintain speed and memory as discussed above. Except for long-term indicators or averages that you may have in your spreadsheet, all indicators will accurately reflect the new contract data.

Another technique that is used in technical analysis systems that does not require getting the historical data for the new contract is to adjust the back contract data up or down by the amount of the discontinuity. You can do this in the spreadsheet by using vacant columns to calculate the adjusted price and then copying the data into the price data columns. Since the price fluctuations are generally about the same for different contract months, the newly calculated indicators will work fine.

Either of these methods for handling the change-over leaves you with a problem if you save your data for later use in long-term detrending analysis or practice trading. The discontinuity at the change-over point remains and can cause problems in later analyses. A way to fix this and generate your own "perpetual" contract is to "blend" the discontinuity. When you copy the new contract data into the spreadsheet, adjust the back contract price data by the amount of the discontinuity in a linearly diminishing fashion over the past 30 to 50 days. Each day's correction is the amount of the discontinuity divided by the number of days over which you are spreading it, times the number of days from the point from where the correction starts. Do the calculation in the spreadsheet, and copy the corrected price data into the price data columns.

3.4 THE RULES AND CHECKLISTS

Just as in chess, the rules are fairly simple, but the application can be difficult and requires good judgment. Good judgment comes from practice.

The foundation for application of the reactivity indicator is determining the dominant price-cycle behavior of the commodity which you wish to trade. Once the detrending analysis is done, and the half-cycle length for the indicator has been selected, the determination of the trade points is usually straightforward. The detrending analysis is not something that is done just once. As discussed earlier, it is a continuing part of the analysis, and adjustments may occasionally be necessary.

For each commodity, you will select a primary indicator for the cycle you wish to trade (usually a cycle with a period in the range of 20 to 30 days) and a short-cycle indicator for a shorter component cycle (usually 1/4 to 1/2 the primary cycle period).

Rule 1: Buy (go long) the commodity when the primary indicator turns up from its low, and sell (go short) the commodity when the indicator turns down from its top.

Adjunct 1: The timing of the trade can be made more precise by using the turn of the short-cycle indicator (data point crosses to smoothed line) at the anticipated primary cycle turning point. The primary indicator must flatten or give some indication of turning.

Adjunct 2: Having entered a trade on the basis of the short-cycle indicator (anticipated turn in the primary), a turn of the short-cycle indicator against the position before the primary indicator has turned, or if there is continuing uncertainty in the primary indicator, close the position.

Rule 2: If the primary indicator has exceeded the critical range, do not reverse the position as the indicator turns.

Adjunct 1: If the critical range is exceeded by less than about 40 percent of the critical range, close (reverse) the position at the next turn in the short-cycle indicator after the short-cycle indicator has penetrated the zero line.

Adjunct 2: If the critical range has been exceeded by more than 40 percent maintain the current position. Add to the position at the next trade point in the same direction. Close (reverse) at the next lower peak (+ or -) in the primary indicator after the primary indicator has reached zero or the short-cycle indicator has penetrated zero twice.

Rule 3: Obey rules 1 and 2. The trading rules are the highest law of the land regarding your trading profits. Don't make trades that are not substantiated by the trading indicators.

Rule 4: Since the rules requiring you to enter a trade do not guarantee a successful trade, be ready to exit a trade if the stop point is exceeded or the indicators turn against your trade.

Adjunct 1: On an opening gap against a position which is near or behind the entry point, close the position 15 to 30 minutes after the opening if the gap has not been filled. Re-enter when the indicators direct.

These rules are simple enough, and their application will become more evident after reviewing the simulated trading in Chapter 5. As with most things in life, the best teacher is experience. When you have done some trading, the application of the rules makes more sense, and you will learn how to handle the grey areas.

To ensure that the rules are being followed and that you haven't forgotten something, it is a good idea to have a checklist that you refer to each day or for each trade. Below are two such lists: one for the mechanics of the trade, and one for the psychological factors.

TRADE CHECKLIST

1. Before the market opens, check the stop-loss points. Either enter stop orders or monitor the market closely and exit any position within about twenty minutes of a stop being hit.

2. Generally, trades should be made late in the day (near the close) when that day's data indicates a trade.

3. Does the primary indicator show the primary cycle is at a turning point? It should turn or show eminent turn, and time must be within reasonable cycle length.

4. Has the short-cycle indicator turned to, or across, its average line?

5. Has either indicator (data and average line) crossed over the critical range line? Has the short-cycle indicator subsequently penetrated zero?

6. Is there a divergence between indicators and price?

7. Verify conditions of Rule 4 just after the opening and just before the close.

PSYCHOLOGICAL CHECKLIST

1. Are the trading rules telling you to make a trade? Do it! If not, don't.

2. Are you hanging on to a position that is against the indicators? This is the hoping and waiting syndrome; exit now!

3. Do you have a preconceived notion of what the market is going to do? Put it out of your mind. Do what the indicators indicate.

4. Commissions are not a factor. If you are wrong now, you're wrong. Exit now, and re-enter when you are right.

5. Don't translate the trade position into dollars. It will affect your emotions and thereby influence your judgment. Think only in terms of the trade, i.e., the indicators.

6. Be particularly vigilant after a period of successful trading. That is when you are most likely to deviate from the rules.

Keep a copy of the rules and the checklist beside your computer and refer to them daily until you are confident that you will not deviate from them. And remember that following all the rules does not mean that every trade will be profitable. But it does mean that you will not make a mistake. Overall, you can make handsome profits.

4

Managing Your Money

. . .

One can make money only if there is real risk based on actual uncertainty, and without uncertainty there is no risk.

Heinz R. Pagels
The Dreams of Reason

There are dozens of technical trading techniques for which it is claimed that wonderful profits can be made. And there are many that will work if properly applied. Some of these techniques may even have some similarities. They are generally at least not contradictory. But in the area of money management in trading, I have found tremendous inconsistencies, and recommended approaches that are exactly opposite.

One can only be concerned and confused when one author advises adding positions as the trade goes your way, and another says start with a given number of contracts and close them out one by one as the trade goes your way. One author says always place a stop-loss (limit stop) order at the time you place your order. Another says never use stop-loss orders.

Perhaps this is an area where personal preference carries the day, but these trade management practices are an extremely important aspect of being successful at this endeavor. You must have a well thought out approach which is systematic and logical, and which answers the questions raised above, as well as a number of others.

Most references that I have found that contain something on money management in trading talk mostly about the use of stop-loss orders. That is one part of money management. Much of our discussion here will also address that subject. An original approach is presented which is systematic and analytical so you will always know where your stop point is, whether it is mental or in the market. But we also need to concern ourselves with where to trade, how much margin to use, when to add contracts to a position, and so on.

4.1 WHERE, WHEN, AND HOW MUCH?

Even if you have a friend in the full-service brokerage business, use a discount broker. The discount brokerage service which I use currently charges commissions which are one-fifth of what I once paid to a full-service broker. You probably already know this because if you're reading this book, it must be because you want to make your own decisions.

What you want is timely execution of your order and accurate statements of what you did; that's all. You don't want someone else making your decision, and you don't want opinions on what you should do. And you don't want your friend to know what you are doing anyway.

Get your data from a daily financial paper or, better yet, from one of many more timely computer database services. Here again, keep it simple. Get only what you need to do your analysis. There is no need for "news" or "hotlines" or numerous government reports. Remember that what we are doing here is technical trading, and all of that is already influencing the data that we are using. And most "expert" analysis is only opinion. It is likely to be contradictory and, most importantly, could put at risk the unbiased, objective interpretation of your indicators.

Even at discount commission rates, you are likely to find that the commissions you've paid are more than a small percentage of your profits. But to the extent possible, you must be able to trade with the feeling that the commissions are not a factor. You must not find yourself hesitating to exit an uncertain position because you are concerned about the commission costs associated with getting out and re-entering later.

The cost of retrieving only the necessary data from a database and the cost of the paper subscription will be negligible. I use an end-of-day download service for commodity futures data that costs $25 per month. Most of the data can be obtained from the cable TV business channel, CNBC, or other local channels.

How Much Margin?

There are two aspects to this question. The first is the size of the account needed to effectively trade, and the second is the amount in that account which is actually committed as margin at any one time.

Conventional wisdom, repeated over and over again in the published literature, is that you should not put money into commodity trading that you are not prepared to lose. That is like saying "Start with the attitude that you are probably going to lose, or that you are going to allow yourself to lose." With visualizations like this, you are programming yourself to lose. That's ludicrous. If you don't have a strategy that can make money, and if you don't have a rigorous system for limiting loses in any one position, then do not trade.

This doesn't mean that you are going to make money as soon as you start trading or that you won't make mistakes resulting in losses. But you must start with a positive attitude and you **must** be disciplined, responsible and cautious **from the start**. With any open position, some portion of your account will always be at risk. It is up to you to make certain that you are limiting that risk by following the system rules; in particular, that you are not letting any losses get large.

There was a time just as I had finished the development of the system presented in this book that I had **all** of my liquid assets in my trading account, and I kept it substantially margined. This was not money that I was prepared to lose, nor did I leave allowance for that to happen.

There are times when you are working within the system that you will accrue losses. If you continue to follow the system, you can expect to get this back. But, if you find that you are taking losses because you are making mistakes, it is best to step back for a moment and evaluate your approach. Take a vacation or paper trade for awhile and follow the system exactly. Then go back and try again.

The size of the account that you start with can be rather modest. It depends upon the margin requirements for the commodities that you choose to trade. It is a good idea to trade commodities from at least three groups, say one grain, one meat, and one financial or metal. If you eliminate the stock index futures which currently have high margins, you can have one or two contracts in each with the margin totaling as little as about $5,000. This is probably the smallest amount your broker will take to open an account. To allow some room for "drawdown," you should add about 30 percent to 50 percent.

It can be difficult to work within the confines of such a small account because of lack of flexibility in margin, but it can be done. An account over $20,000 is comfortable.

Drawdown is that amount that becomes unavailable for margin because of open positions that are behind the entry point, and accrued actual losses that have occurred from the point of highest balance. Using this definition, the allowance for drawdown at any time is the excess in the account over that allocated to margin for contracts that you are trading or intend to trade.

This gets right into the second question, which is, "how much of the account balance is to be committed to margin at any one time?" If we never took a loss, we could use 100 percent of the account balance for margin. This would be the most aggressive approach possible and would provide maximum gain. But you do have to be able to accept losses without having your broker call for more margin, so you cannot fully margin the balance.

Yet, to maximize the possible gain, you would like to leverage the account as far as prudently possible. However, if you have taken some losses while trading your chosen size of position, you do not want to have to reduce the size of the positions while making up these losses with good trades. It is important to be able to continue to trade the same size position to make up the loss on the next good trade. Therefore, the drawdown allowance must consider the extreme probabilities for a number of consecutive losses, and the size of the average gain relative to the average loss.

This becomes a matter of your personal trading performance. In trading studies, with strict adherence to the rules of the system in this book, and particularly the limiting of losses, I have found that 40 percent of the available balance is sufficient excess margin over that allocated to trade positions. This applies to a diversified account trading four or more commodities, and with roughly equal amounts of the margin allocated to each. Therefore, based on this past performance, we can utilize margin up to 60 percent of the available balance. The available balance is the total equity, that is, the sum of segregated funds and equity in open positions that is secure beyond the stop point.

As the account size increases, the procedure is to periodically, perhaps monthly, determine the approximate available balance and allocate it about equally to the number of commodities that you trade. This provides a guideline for the number of contracts that will comprise your position for each commodity.

This approach makes full use of the capital while maintaining some room for drawdown without margin calls. You won't always have full positions in all the commodities that you trade, but this allocation defines the **maximum**. You may wish to do something less, particularly early in your trading experience.

There is another limit on the number of contracts that you will carry. That is the "comfort limit." The more contracts, the larger the magnitude of the risk, the bigger the swings in the value of your position, and so on. This is a real limit and one to which you must pay attention. Don't push your comfort zone too hard. That can cause excessive stress, and stress leads to trading errors. If the balance in the account is considered as just a number used for keeping score, devoid of emotional content, then the comfort level does not limit you.

What about when things aren't going well, and you get a margin call notice? There is only one simple answer. Do not send money. Close a position. Then go back and review your trading practices relative to the the rules of the method. In particular, look again at the section, "Limiting Your Losses." If you're in this situation, you made a mistake. You either put on too many contracts or you obviously have some loser that should already have been closed.

Adding to Your Position

For most short-term trading, this is not something with which you need to be concerned. If you are using daily data to trade a cycle with a period of less than about 30 days, then the basic approach is that a trade signal requires that you trade the number of contracts that you have allocated to this particular commodity. You will always put on this same position until your account balances changes and you reallocate margin, or your comfort level changes.

The only rationale for adding contracts to a position is if a shorter term indicator gives a subsequent trade signal. This presupposes that the trade is going in your favor, and there is available margin. For a primary trading cycle period of less than 25 days, it is unlikely that there is a reliable shorter term indicator based on daily data. You can use hourly data in a shorter term indicator, such as momentum or stochastics, to add contracts at bottoms of shorter term cycles if you have a clearly identified cycle.

It is not uncommon for a commodity price to "retest" a top or a bottom at a primary cycle turning point. If this occurs after you have put on your position, and the primary indicator continues to indicate that the trade is correct, this can be a good time to add to a position. This would be indicated by the short-cycle indicator.

For commodities that tend to be more strongly trending, that is, the longer cycles are more dominant, it can be advantageous to trade the longer cycle and add to the position using a short cycle. This minimizes the risk in the early, more uncertain, part of the trend and still allows maximizing profits by utilizing the margin generated by the trade as it proceeds in your direction. For this to work well the long cycle needs to typically be comprised of four or more shorter cycles. Since you are trading half-cycles (long going up and short going down), this gives you one or two chances to add.

Another time to add to a position is the case where the primary reactivity indicator has exceeded the critical range by more than 40 percent (see rule two, adjunct two) and you have maintained your position. You can add contracts as the indicator again turns to enter the next cycle.

When adding contracts at subsequent short cycle points, add only the number of the original position or less. Assuming the price has moved in your direction, this limits the risk position to that of the added trade since your stop-loss exit point would maintain the previous contracts at about break even or better.

4.2 LIMITING YOUR LOSSES

Limiting losses is probably the toughest and most crucial part of trading success. We need to know how, where and when to exit a trade which is working against us.

"How" is not just picking up the phone and placing the order. It is learning to overcome all of the psychological barriers to admitting you're wrong and taking a loss; both of which are sometimes difficult. "Where" to exit is told by the indicators and backed up by the stop-loss point that we will discuss below. "When" is usually right now.

The trading methods are not perfect; they only get the probabilities in your favor. Therefore, you will frequently find yourself in a trade that is going the wrong way. Your first recourse always is to update and examine your trading indicators, and take any actions indicated. In addition, you should have a point beyond which you exit regardless of the indicators.

Conventional trading wisdom has the slogan "cut your losses and let your profits run." That, in itself, is about as helpful as "buy low, sell high." Exactly, how do you do this? Also, conventional trading wisdom, and most actual practice, is to always use a stop-loss order.

A great deal has been written on the use of stop-loss orders in commodity trading. No discussion on trading commodities would be complete without it. This discussion is included here because it is commonly considered to be part of money management, much the same as asset allocation might be, but it is really part of a trading strategy. The advice in the literature varies from always placing your stop-loss order at the same time you place your entry order to never using stops. And if you decide to use stops, I have not been able to find a consistent and logical set of rules published about where to place them.

Stop-Loss Orders

Let's examine this question of using stop-loss orders (these are really stop-limit orders) and see whether or not it makes sense to use them, and then develop a rational way of determining where the limit point is based upon market behavior.

It appears that the use of stop-loss orders is as much a matter of individual style as the trading methods themselves. And that is how it should be. The use of stop-loss orders should be an integral part of the trading strategy. The challenge is to determine their use based on your trading style, and to determining the exit point.

In my early trading experience in commodities, the majority of my losses were caused by untimely triggering of stop-loss orders. This was the major factor in preventing me from achieving an overall profit. I would enter a trade (with the normal lack of confidence of a relative novice), place my stop based on some indefinite guidelines, or what I felt comfortable with as a loss, and then see that stop get filled just as the market turned and proceeded in the direction of the original trade.

And the matter is further complicated by the miss of the trade. You could, of course, re-enter the trade when the market turns, but this is not easy to do, especially for a beginner lacking confidence. You are trading from a position of uncertainty anyway, and after the market has gone against you and stopped you out, the uncertainty levels will likely be high enough to make you hesitant to re-enter the market. That's where you lose your opportunity.

An obvious solution is not to use stops at all, but rather make your exit by making a conscious decision based upon market behavior. As your experience increases and your confidence grows, you will move in this direction. But you may like to know that, although the majority of early losses were from stops being filled even though I was right about the trade, by far the largest individual losses occurred when I didn't use stops.

So, it seems there should be some system for this stop-loss business which works best. Both extremes in the use of stops, either always or never, are likely to be wrong for you. However, if you are a floor trader you would be toward the never extreme; if you trade longer term and do not devote significant time to following the market during the day, you should probably be in the "always" group.

Reasons to Use Stops

Consider some of the reasons that stop-loss orders are used:

    a. Insure against a major loss.
    b. Automatic exit from a profitable trade when the market turns.
    c. Entering a market based on a price break past a certain point.
    d. Relieve you of decision-making responsibility.
    e. Psychological comfort.

Although the first three appear valid and are the usual reasons given, the last two are probably the real reasons for many traders. These are not mutually exclusive but should give you reason to think. Steidlmayer (1986) says the use of stops is an excuse not to monitor market behavior and make conscious decisions based on an understanding of what the market is telling you.

For a short-term trader particularly, I believe his evaluation is correct. You enter the market based on your knowledge of what the market is doing (based on raw data and derived data), and you should exit it the same way. Within the rules of the reactivity system, a stop-limit computed as described below would get executed infrequently. But I also recognize that this assumes an ideal human that is ever alert and not subject to hampering emotional characteristics which may cause you to sometimes break the rules.

If you are trading without an on-line quote system or cannot devote full attention to the market, it is not likely that you can always make the "considered" trade. The key is that these stops must protect you, i.e., work to your advantage. They must be strategically placed.

First and foremost, they are insurance. You don't expect to have them executed, but they can protect you from sudden unexpected happenings. You may place the stop-loss order to protect yourself, but if your trade is wrong based on what the data is telling you, get out now; don't just wait for the stop to get hit, hoping the market will turn before it happens.

Always remember the basis of your trading. You enter the trade because the weight of evidence leads you to conclude that the market will not move in the opposite direction. Going your direction is great, not going anywhere is fine. Free exposure is all you ask. If you trade in this manner, exit when the evidence has changed, and let your stop provide insurance against the occasional surprise.

Recognize that making the decision to exit a trade is likely to be more difficult than the studied decision to enter. It's human nature. You've carefully reviewed and studied the indicators and made the move. Now, are you going to easily admit that you were wrong? Probably not.

Remember that you entered the trade objectively, and if it turns out that it was wrong, you must exit the same way. If you can't admit you were wrong when the evidence says so, you are going to be even more wrong later. It is this difficulty in remaining objective about the trade that leads to reason (d) above; i.e., relief from decision-making responsibility.

Reason (e) is a valid one and goes hand in hand with (a). It lets you sleep at night and allows you a degree of certainty which can lower the stress levels associated with trading.

Reasons (b) and (c) are generally not valid uses of stop-loss orders in the reactivity system. The principal reason is that they consider only price. All other information is ignored. Your knowledge of what is occurring based on the indicators we've discussed should allow you to make more advantageous entry and exit points than tripping a certain price level. As always, there are exceptions, and it may depend on your individual approach.

A useful application of (b) are those times when you are consciously willing to get less than maximum profit from a trade, and you want to "walk away." Use a trailing stop capturing most of the profit, and go fishing.

There is at least one rule regarding stop-loss orders; don't allow the security of being able to use a stop-loss order entice you into making trades you're really not sure about. The numerous small losses will consume your profits.

Reasons to Not Use Stop-Loss Orders

Short-term traders (who presumably closely monitor the markets) should consider not placing stop-loss orders (use mental stop points only). The main reason is that almost invariably, you will have an opportunity to exit at a better price sometime soon after the stop point has been hit.

The market by its nature is always auctioning up and down over a range within the trend. At the end of one of these extremes is where your stop gets filled. Generally, assuming you have followed all the indicators and market behavior in entering your trade, the point where your stop takes you out is really the point where you should be considering adding to your position.

Perhaps this level of discipline or objectivity is an almost unreasonable expectation of yourself. The normal behavior in the case of a mental stop-loss point is that after the point has been reached, and the market bounces back, you give a sigh of relief, relax and start hoping. You don't take that opportunity to exit because now it's going your way. When your mental stop-loss point has been reached, you must review what you now know, and if the trade is uncertain, you **must** exit until you are certain.

4.3 COMPUTING THE STOP-LOSS POINT

If you have done some trading, you know that the only stressful thing about trading is having a position that is going against you. Obviously, these are to be avoided. But, sometimes you are in a position that is consistent in all respects with the indicators, but for the short-term (usually intraday) is going the wrong way. You may be in just a little early, or you may be wrong. The indicators are not always right. To what point do you stay with this trade before getting out?

Other times you may have a good trade, and the indicators have not yet turned telling you to get out (technical indicators are generally lagging), but some significant change in fundamentals causes a rapid reversal in price. At what point do you protect your profit?

We need rational answers to these questions. We need to know at all times a point beyond which the probabilities favor a continued move in the other direction. Most of the time, by just following the indicators as presented you will know when to get out, or to reverse, but sometimes a more timely technique is needed. And, if you don't monitor the markets closely, you need to know where to put the trailing stop.

Commonly suggested points are just beyond previous short-term highs or lows, or perhaps, at some fixed dollar amount beyond your entry point. Using previous short-term highs and lows is sometimes right but has two disadvantages. First, since this is a common practice, these become areas of bunched stop-limit orders. When these are triggered, it can push the market right through all the stops causing a spike which takes you out with significant slippage, and at which point the market may reverse, and you want to be back in. Second, your point of entry may be such that a previous high or low may be unnecessarily far away, or too close.

Another common approach of setting stop points is to set the risk as a fraction of expected reward. This is only an academic exercise because you cannot foretell the future; you do not know what the potential reward is on any given trade. Choosing a stop point as a percentage of margin or a fixed dollar amount is obviously arbitrary and not related to market behavior.

What we are going to do here is develop a method for computing the proper stop-loss point for tomorrow after the close of the market today. The stop-loss point, that is, the point at which it becomes probable that the market is going still further against your trade, is a function of market volatility. As volatility determines potential gain, so does it determine the potential risk. The starting point for determining the appropriate stop point is to determine a measure of intraday or short-term volatility. We need to separate the noise from the trend.

A good measure of short-term volatility is the average trading range, such as the average daily range. To make this as responsive as possible to the most recent data, compute this as an exponential average of the daily range using an appropriate smoothing constant consistent with the cycle period that you are trading.

We also need a measure of the likely variation of the range beyond the average value. Assuming a normal distribution, we can compute the standard deviation (a statistical function available on many calculators and in computer spreadsheet programs). By its definition, a one standard deviation variation on both sides of the mean will provide a 78 percent probability that the value will fall within that range. A multiple of the standard deviation can be applied to take in a higher percentage as required.

Now you can begin to see that if we can extend the expected price range to the next day, then we can infer that if the price extends beyond the extreme of that range in a direction against our position, that there is a high probability that our trade is wrong, and we should be out. That is, it is wrong for now. Re-check the indicators; you may have the right idea but you were in early, and you'll have a chance for a better entry later.

The only thing still needed is a reasonable assumption of the point around which prices will vary tomorrow based on what has happened up through the close today. We can get this by extrapolating an exponential average of the daily midpoint.

The generalized analytical form for computing the stop-loss points is provided in Appendix B. The basic procedure is to first compute a trailing exponential average of the daily midpoint using a responsive smoothing factor of, say 0.4. Then, for simplicity, assume that tomorrow's midpoint is given by the smoothed midpoint of today.

Once a short-term trend is established, this midpoint will move in the direction of that trend. Having this point, we then need to know how far above is appropriate for a stop-loss point for a short position, or how far below the midpoint is appropriate for a stop-loss for a long position. The probable extreme for tomorrow's price movement away from the midpoint is given by the sum of 1/2 the average daily range plus a factor times the standard deviation.

The average daily range is computed as a trailing exponential average using a smoothing factor approximately equivalent to 1/2 the length of the cycle that you are trading. For an approximate 30-day cycle, use an equivalent of a 15-day average, i.e., 0.13. The standard deviation for the daily range is also computed over a number of days in a half-period. Then in the absence of a change of trend, the probable maximum distance, D, from the midpoint is:

$$D = \frac{\overline{R}_d}{2} + k \cdot \sigma$$

where: $\overline{R}_d$ is the exponentially averaged daily range,
  k is a factor between 1.8 and 2.5,
  and, σ is the standard deviation.

The stop point for a long position, S_l, is:

$$S_l = M - D$$

where, M, is the extended midpoint. The stop point for a short position is:

$$S_s = M + D$$

I further smooth these stop-loss points by using them as a exponential average with a smoothing factor of 0.5.

The constant, k, is a multiplier for the standard deviation to adjust the probability for tomorrow's expected range to stay within the limits. I have found it best to determine this empirically by examining data for the commodity you are trading and pick a value which keeps the stop point just out of range of the typical pull-backs in price **within the trend** that you are trading. Typically, a value of 2.0 to 2.75 works well with the smaller value giving a closer stop.

If your trade is correct, there is a high probability that tomorrow's price will not go against you beyond the stop point. If it does, you should certainly re-examine your indicators and/or exit the position.

An example of how this computed stop point tracks with price is shown in Figure 4-1 for cotton for the last half of 1988. The value of k was set at 1.8 for this computation giving a closely following stop. The price band shown is formed by the daily high and low price. The computed stop point for both long and short positions is shown by the line with symbols.

Obviously this method provided excellent guidance for placing trailing stop orders or maintaining mental stop points. There is only one point where the stop would have been hit when the trend was still strongly down, and that is on day 153. The price came just to the long stop point on day 241. These limits can be loosened as you see fit by adjusting the value of k.

Normal entry and exit (or reversing) of trades is done using the reactivity indicators, and these stop points are protection against any sizable unexpected losses. However, you can see that in the case of cotton just using these stop points as trade points would have been very profitable.

Hopefully, with proper consideration of the trading parameters, you can get your trade into the correct day. It's not likely that you're also going to pick the right minute. On the entry day the stop point as computed above is not likely to be applicable since its smoothing causes a day or so delay and you hopefully entered near a market extreme. Here you can find a stop point by adding 1/2 the average daily range plus about two times the standard deviation to the midpoint of the entry day's range. As an alternate, place your stop beyond the previous short-term price extreme by about 20 percent of the average daily range.

As an additional rule of thumb; if you have legitimately held a position through a short-cycle top or bottom after the turn at which you en-

Figure 4–1   Stop-Loss Points—Cotton

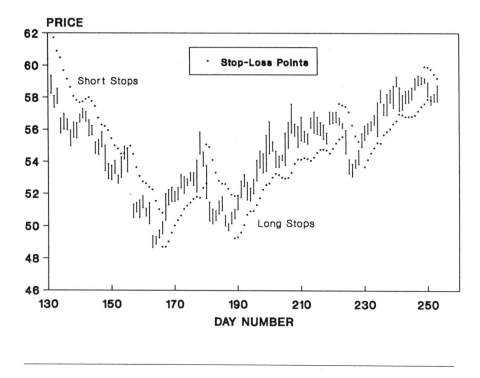

tered, plan on setting a stop-loss that gets you out at near break-even as you go onto the next short cycle, regardless of the computed stop-loss point. If the market hasn't moved much to that point, it is generally not worth risking a loss. Look for the opportunity to trade your primary cycle in the other direction.

5

Simulated Real Trading

. . .

The obscure we see eventually, the completely apparent takes longer.

Edward R. Murrow
Broadcaster

Earlier in this book, as well as in others you may read, you will find that the real data examples given to illustrate application of technical concepts or a new indicator somehow always seem to provide superb results. These results may not be typical because the author picks the particular time period in which the indicators worked well. Real life isn't always so kind and may provide experience which is . . . more diverse, shall we say?

In this chapter, we are going to pick an arbitrary time period—the first 90 days of 1989—and trade five different commodity futures during that period (180 days for Eurodollars). In each case, we will trade them based on the indicators presented in previous chapters and get a look at the kinds of typical behavior that you will encounter and how it is interpreted. The commodities traded include examples from the major groups: grains (wheat), meats (live hogs), metals (copper), fibers (cotton), and financials (Eurodollars).

Study of this section is an important part of learning to trade with the methods developed in this book. Here you can get experience with how the rules are applied and how the trade decisions are made. After you are trading by this method, it will be worthwhile to occasionally refer back to this section as a "refresher."

Realize also as you study these trades, that the cycles chosen for use here are based on data leading up to and including the period studied, and all the discussion is in present tense. These cycles are not necessarily constant, and you may find from your detrending studies that there has been some change in the cycle content, and the half-period length for the indicators may need to be adjusted. That is an important aspect of this method since it allows for adapting to changes in market behavior. These markets have remained remarkably consistent, however, and as this goes to press, I have not found it necessary to make any changes for wheat, live hogs and copper, and only some minor changes for cotton and Eurodollars.

For the sample trading below, it is assumed that the account equity balance is about $40,000. In keeping with the discussion in Chapter 4, we will allocate half this amount as usable margin, so about $4,000 can be allocated to each of five commodities. Commissions will be taken as $25 round turn. At the end of the discussion for each commodity, a summary of profits and losses is given. For consistency, the positions coming into the period are marked-to-market (MTM) at the close of the previous day, and the positions going out are MTM at the close of the last day.

As you prepare to study each of the commodities, refer back to the trading rules and the checklists in Section 3.4. Also, as you study the trade points for each commodity, refer back to the graphs of the price and the indicators to get the full visual picture of what is going on. It may get tedious, but it will help you visualize in actual trading experience. And it may be best to study one of the commodities at a time while you are also doing real-time actual or paper trading.

The trade position coming into each trade point is given to the right of the trade point heading.

5.1 CHICAGO WHEAT

There are three cycle lengths to follow for trading wheat. However, for each commodity, one cycle is chosen as the primary cycle to trade and a shorter cycle is used to make the trade in a more timely manner. In rough numbers, the wheat cycles are about 10, 30 and 120 trading days. There is a weak, approximately 15-day influence, and another that is about 60 days (12 weeks), but they are secondary.

From studies of the last eight years of daily price data, the cycles are more accurately described as:

8.5 days, standard deviation = 2.3 (27%)
29 days, standard deviation = 3.2 (11%)
115 days, standard deviation = 14 (13%)

Keep in mind that the standard deviation means that about 78 percent of the time the cycle length will fall within + or - one standard deviation. Cycle lengths can vary outside these ranges.

The longer term trend is given by the 115 day cycle. This is an approximate semi-annual cycle which tends to come in combination of one longer and one shorter cycle each year. As an exception to the normal procedure of measuring cycle lengths from bottom to bottom, the 115-day cycle in wheat seems best (so far) measured from top to top.

For trading wheat, I have chosen the 29-day cycle as the primary cycle. The short 8.5-day is more variable, as short cycles usually are, but it can be used with caution as a timing cycle to improve trade points. The 115-day cycle is primarily for reference and can be used to resolve uncertainties in trend.

For trading these cycles, we need indicators of roughly half the length of the short end of the range of each cycle. I use a simple 4-day momentum (trading indicator), a 12-day reactivity (primary indicator) and a 55-day momentum. Since the primary indicator for wheat is the 12-day, you need to use the reactivity calculation for this; you can use simple momentums for the other cycles just to simplify the calculations.

The daily midpoint and the MF indicator is used to watch for divergences as a confirmation of a trend change.

In keeping with the rules given in section 3.4, the basic trading rules for wheat are:

1. The 12-day primary indicator is in a time period where the 29-day cycle top or bottom may be anticipated, and it shows an indication of turning.

2. The 4-day indicator data point has come to, or crossed, its exponential average.

The daily high and low for wheat is shown in Figure 5–1. Also shown on this graph are the long and short stop-loss points as computed by the method given in Chapter 4. The primary indicator, the 12-day reactivity, is shown in Figure 5–2, the 4-day indicator in Figure 5–3, and daily price midpoint and money flow index (M/MF) are shown in Figure 5–4. These are the basic pieces of information needed for determining trade points. As you will see, there are times when some other information may be considered to enhance your judgment, but working only with the price and the three indicators shown works well.

One contract for wheat is 5,000 bushels, and unlike other commodities, trades are made in bushels rather than number of contracts. When you tell your broker to sell "five wheat" you're selling 5,000 bushels, or one contract. The margin for wheat at my broker at the time of this trading was $850 per contract, so we will assume a normal trade of five contracts (25,000 bu.).

It will be much easier to follow the discussion of the trade points if you make copies of Figures 5-1 through 5-4 and lay them out where you can refer to them more easily.

Trade Point 1: Day 10   (Short: 5 contracts)

The position carried as we come into the period is a short of five contracts. Based on the timing of the previous 29-day cycle bottom, the next cycle bottom is expected between day 5 and 15. The little recovery in price on day nine gets our attention. The 4-day indicator has come back almost to its average line and the 12-day data point has come up. You could trade at this point, but caution would dictate letting the 4-day come to, or cross, its average line.

On day 10, the price drops below the previous day's low early in the day, but holds above the low of day eight, indicating support. Day 10 is trade day. Late in the trading day, analysis of the data shows the 4-day across its exponential smoothing line and the 12-day still indicating a possible turn. The trade is made at $4.02-1/2. Wheat trades are normally quoted in cents per bushel and trade in increments of 1/4 cent, so in the following discussion, this would be shown as 402.50.

Figure 5-1 Wheat Futures Price

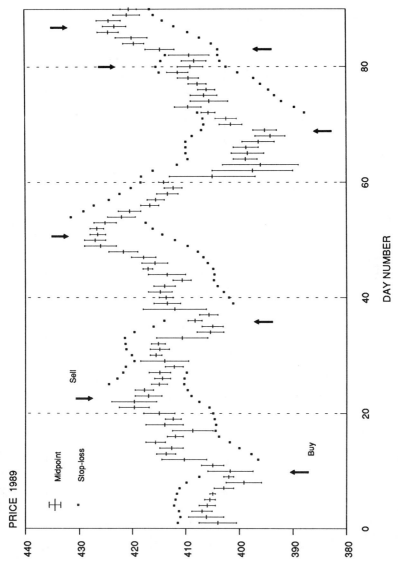

Figure 5-2   12-Day Reactivity

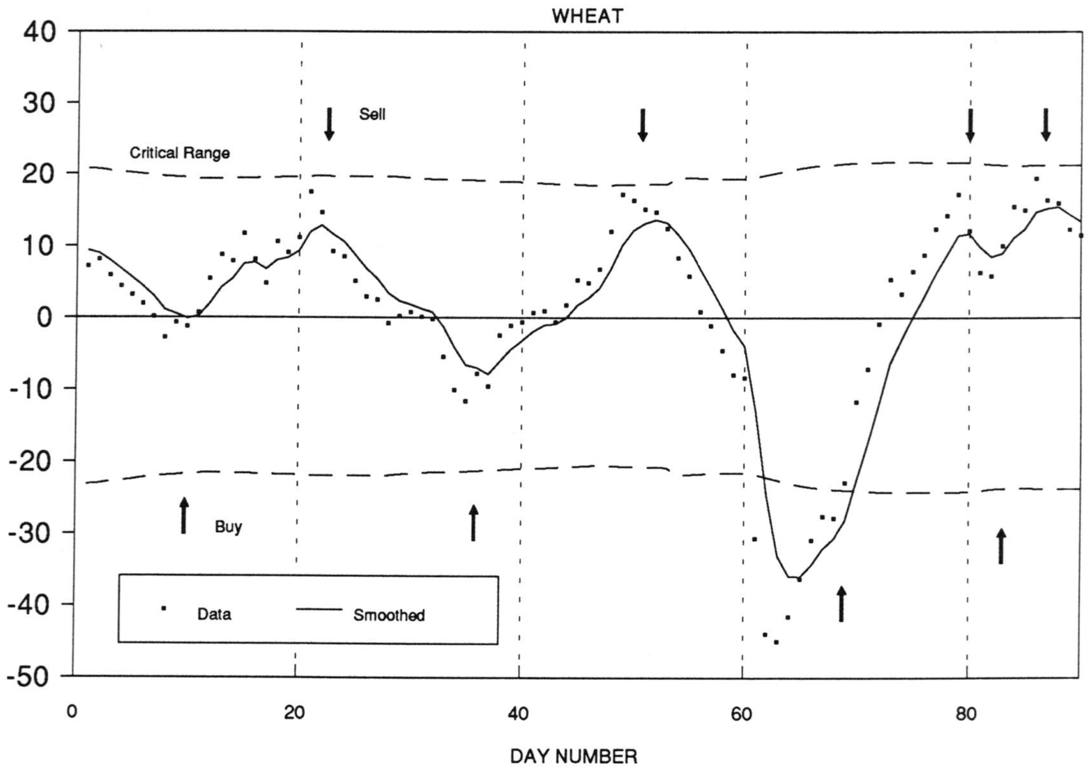

Figure 5–3   4-Day Momentum

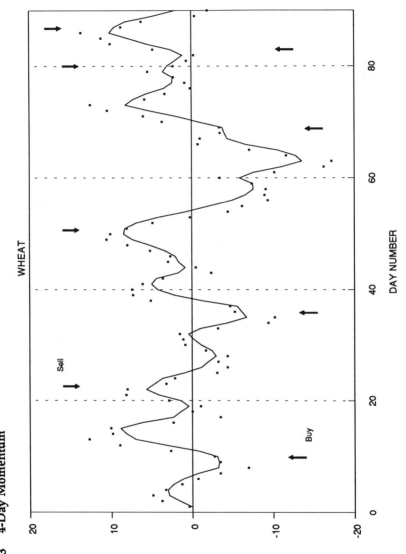

Figure 5-4 Midpoint and Money Flow

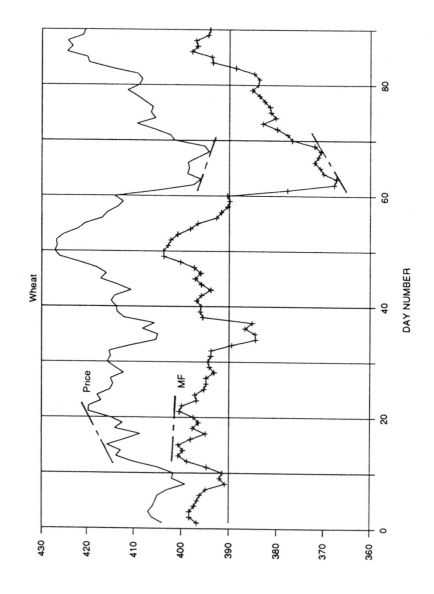

Just to consider some alternatives, if the trade had been made on day 9 it probably could have been made at about 402. You would have worried on day 10 as the price dropped. The small improvement in entry price is probably not worth the additional risk and stress.

You don't really know the day's range until the day is over. However, an hour or two into trading on day 10 you would have seen the higher low hold, and you could have plugged in the low and the average daily range and seen that this was likely the time to trade. You could have made the trade earlier in the day and gained about two cents per bushel. This would have been a justified risk since there was evidence of the indicators turning and there was evidence of support for the price. For purposes here, we will not assume that level of aggressiveness or involvement. We will take the trade at 402.50 and note that the initial stop-loss point would be about 396.50.

At this trade point we offset the five contract short position and put on a five contract long position; a total buy order of "50 wheat" (10 contracts). This trade was "Marked-to-Market" at the close on day 0 at 405.25, so there was a gross profit of 2.75 cents per bushel. Each contract of 5,000 bushels is worth $50 for each cent change in price, resulting in a gross profit of $687.50. Since commissions are "round turn," for this trade coming in we will deduct commissions off the position going out on day 90.

Trade Point 2: Day 23   (Long: 5 Contracts)

The price trades up for a few days and reverses as would be expected to complete the short-term cycle. As the price recovers again after day 20 we see some conditions setting up for a topping in price. By day 22 we see the *potential* for divergences between the price and the short-term indicator, and in the midpoint and money flow, M/MF.

It is important to note "potential" divergences, because a divergence doesn't exist until a turn is made. As day 22 ends, the divergences seem to be in place but the criteria for the 4-day indicator turning to or across its average line has clearly not been met. On day 23, the price trades lower, and it is clear that it is time to trade. The 12-day and 4-day indicators drop; the 4-day showing a clear divergence with price between day 15 and day 22 (compare Figures 5-1 and 5-3). Estimating the volume and change in open interest at about their average values (since we won't have their actual values until the next day) we can calculate and see the divergence in the M/MF.

The position is reversed (offset long and go short) on day 23 at 416.50, so having entered at 402.50 gives a gross profit of 14 cents per bushel or $700/contract. Allowing $25 per contract commission, the net profit on our five contracts is $3,375.

Trade Point 3: Day 36   (Short: 5 Contracts)

Having reversed at trade point 2, we are now short 5 contracts and expecting a bottom somewhere in the neighborhood of day 38, plus or minus about 5 (last bottom was day 9). The trade signal comes on day 36 and we buy 10 contracts at 407.25. The profit on the short position is 9.25/bushel, $462.50 for each contract and totaling $2,187.50 after commissions.

We are now long and on day 37, the market sells off to a low of 404 and then recovers. This behavior is typical as the price makes a further test of the old trend before turning. If you are conservative, you just sit through this, and be a little nervous. If you are more aggressive and monitor the market fairly closely, you see this as a further opportunity. Near the end of the day, you see that the 4-day indicator continues higher, the 12-day continues to show a possible turn, and the price holds a higher bottom. If you have the margin, this is a good time to add to the position, otherwise ignore it. Here we will continue being conservative.

Trade Point 4: Day 51   (Long: 5 Contracts)

The price continues up nicely, through the short-term cycle bottom at day 43 and then swiftly up to a high on day 49 of 428. The price is held by resistance at 428 again on day 50. This is exactly the midpoint of the cycle period, and the top can be expected. The trade is signaled on day 51 by the short-cycle indicator, and the sale is made at 426.25 (close long and go short). The long position profit is 19 cents per bushel, $950/contract, netting $4,625 after commissions.

Trade Point 5: Day 69   (Short: 5 Contracts)

The position is now short, and prices are dropping. The next anticipated low would be in the time frame around day 65. We get concerned on day 60 because we have a nice profit, and the 4-day indicator reverses as the price does a slight recovery. If this were the 30-day cycle bottom, it would be a short cycle; not impossible, but notice that the 12-day is well below its average line and has not indicated a turn. We wait, and we are rewarded nicely. In the next three days, the price collapses as the long-term trendliners are stopped out, and the price hits a low of 389.

Handling of the next trade and the behavior of this market between days 60 and 70 merits some discussion. It represents an exception where following rule two and its adjuncts will cause the miss of a good trade. The behavior of most markets in the area where the primary indicator has exceeded the critical range is the most difficult. Rule two is a good guideline, and at the least requires that some solid evidence be available before exception is taken.

The 12-day reactivity clearly breaks significantly below the lower critical range, and exceeds the range by more than 40 percent. Rule two, adjunct two, says hold the current position. You do not reverse your position because there is a high probability that prices will again be at least this low or lower within the next cycle period.

The behavior to this point would lead you to expect, under normal conditions, that this market would remain weak, possibly until a higher bottom occurs in the 12-day indicator. I will note here that the price did again return to this level on day 105, making the critical range penetration a valid indication, but there was a good trading opportunity in between which will simply be missed in this case. A missed trade within the context of your system, although disappointing, is within perfectly good trading practice; a good point to remember.

In this case, the short position will be held through the initial bottom, but by day 69 the data warrants a critical review and a decision needs to be made. A number of indications accompany this circumstance which gives sufficient cause to revert to the first backup position; rule two, adjunct one, and make the prudent decision to exit the short on day 69:

1. The price midpoint and the 4-day indicator show a clear divergence on day 68 while the 12-day reactivity data point does not go up.

2. As the price recovers on day 69, there is a significant divergence between the price midpoint and the MF (Figure 5-4) indicating major participation in the market on the long side.

3. You would notice as you examine the data (not shown), that the open interest declined steadily and substantially on days 55 through 62. This indicated a lot of long positions being covered as the price declined. This type of covering usually drives markets to extreme conditions.

This last item is a judgment factor which is not specific in the indicators but is part of extracting information that the market is giving you.

Evaluation of this factor is helped by knowing that the wheat market had made substantial gains through the last half of 1988, having increased more than a dollar per bushel. The market makes its top on day 50 of 1989. There is tremendous long open interest. As the price breaks below about 410 on day 61, there is high selling pressure as the longs scramble to get out.

Not knowing, of course, of the rally to come, and remaining within rule two, the position would not be reversed and we would wait for the next opportunity to go short again. The short is closed on day 69 at 396. This trade yielded 30.25/bu, $1512.50/contract, and a net of $7,437.50 on five contracts.

Trade Point 6: Day 80   (No Position)

The next sell signal comes on day 80. It is barely within the half-cycle window, but because of the previous penetration of the lower critical range by the 12-day reactivity, we have reason to believe we are still in a down-trending market in which the cycle tops come early in the cycle. The short position is taken at 409.

Trade Point 7: Day 83   (Short: 5 Contracts)

As can be seen in Figure 5-1, the stop on the short position should be at 414. This stop gets hit on day 83 as the market rallies. Even though all the indicators turn up, this is at an expected cycle top and not a time to take a long position. The loss on the short position is five cents/bu or $250/contract, giving a total loss after commissions of ($1375) on the five contracts.

Trade Point 8: Day 87   (No Position)

The market rallies to probe the previous high (day 50) and hits 426.50 on day 86. Day 87 brings the sell signal, and the short position is taken at 425 as the market rallies toward the close. This point is late in the cycle for a top; there is an apparent divergence on the midpoint/money flow, the 4-day indicator has turned down, and the 12-day is making a top. On day 88, the price tests the top of 426.50 and is turned back. Re-checking the indicators shows that this would be an excellent time to add to (or double) the position.

As mentioned above, the penetration of the lower critical range by the 12-day reactivity between days 60 and 70 indicated the retracement of any subsequent rally. This did in fact occur, and the short position taken on day 87 and 88 would be closed at 395 on day 106 for a pleasing profit. Unfortunately, that is outside the time range for this example; so we must mark-to-market on day 90 (420.50) and show the net on the short position of $1,000, (425.0–420.5) × 250–125.

Wrap-up on Wheat

Now let's summarize the 90-day period and look at the results. The eight trades are listed in Table 5-1, and a summary of the results is shown in Figure 5-5.

This is a good record considering there was never more than about $4,000 margin required (five contracts), and the one loss was small. It is worth going back and studying again to become familiar with the patterns. Cover the graphs with a piece of paper; sliding it from left to right, and only look at what you would actually see at each trade point.

5.2 LIVE HOGS

The primary cycle for trading hogs is the six-to-eight week cycle. It averages about 36 trading days and can vary from 30 to 45. The seasonal cycles are also of interest because trading with the seasonal trend improves the profits, and at times of strong seasonal tendencies, larger positions can be considered. The seasonal variation is semiannual; prices make lows in the spring, usually February to April, and again in the fall, around October. The highest prices are in the summer, usually July and August. These seasonal tendencies are reflected in the prices of the corresponding contract months, but they still can influence the shorter term cycles.

Two shorter term cycles (less than 30 days) are apparent, but they are more variable. At times, a 12- to 16-day cycle will exert some influence but it is not consistent and many times absent. There is a short cycle that can be used to enter and exit at expected turns in the 36-day cycle. It is quite variable between five and eight days, but is a good short-term timing aid.

There are four graphs of data and indicators that are used to trade hogs:

- the price and the computed stop-loss points (Figure 5–6),

- the 18-day reactivity for the 30- to 45-day cycle (Figure 5–7),

- the 4-day reactivity for the short-term cycle (Figure 5–8),

- the price midpoint and money flow, MF, (Figure 5–9.

Table 5–1   Wheat Trading Summary

Trade	Buy	Sell	Quan.	Buy @	Sell @	Net
	day # (tp)			cents/bu		($)
Short	10 (1)	0 (MTM)	5	402.50	405.25	687.50
Long	10 (1)	23.(2)	5	402.50	416.50	3,375.00
Short	36 (3)	23 (2)	5	407.25	416.50	2,187.50
Long	36 (3)	51 (4)	5	407.25	426.25	4,635.00
Short	69 (5)	41 (4)	5	396.00	426.25	7,437.50
Short	SO 83 (7)	80 (6)	5	414.00	409.00	(1,375.00)
Short	90 (MTM)	87 (8)	5	420.50	425.00	1,000.00
		TOTAL				$17,937.50
		Average per contract				3,587.50

*Notes: (tp)—Trade point number: MTM—Marked to market; SO—Stopped out; Commission is $25 / contract round turn (not taken on incoming position, but is taken on out-going position).

Figure 5–5   Trading Profits—Wheat

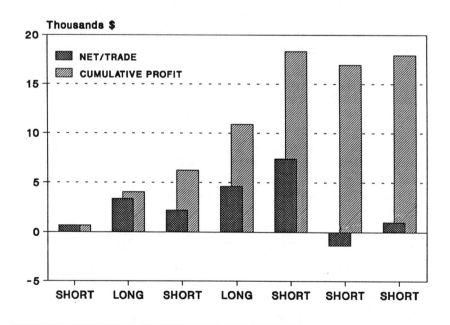

Figure 5–6   Live Hog Futures Price

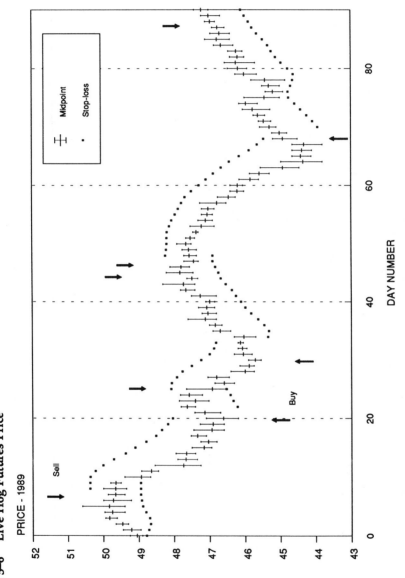

PRICE - 1989

Midpoint

Stop-loss

Sell

Buy

DAY NUMBER

Figure 5-7   18-Day Reactivity—Live Hogs

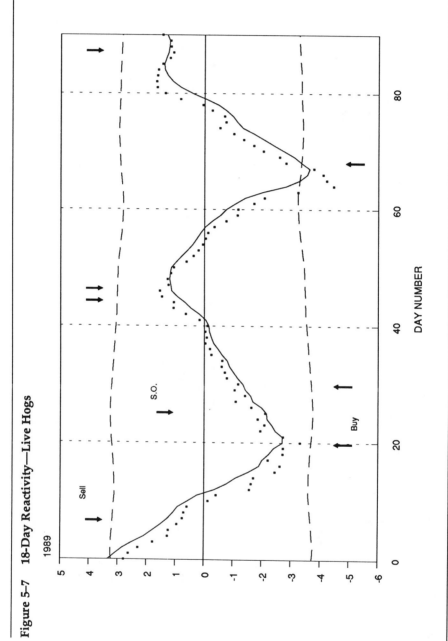

Figure 5–8   4-Day Reactivity—Live Hogs

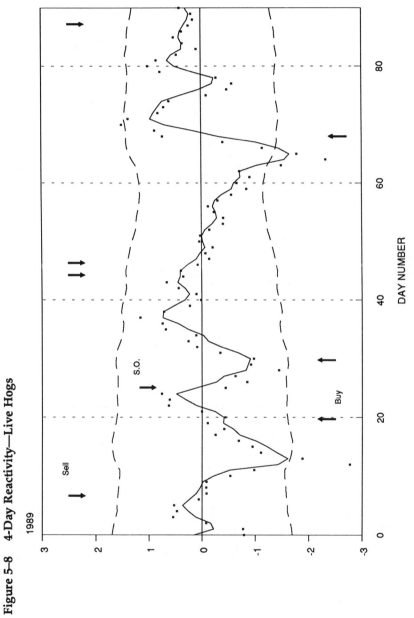

Figure 5–9 Midpoint and Money Flow

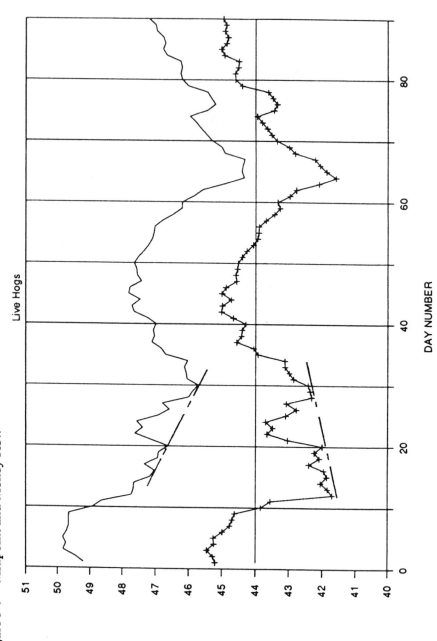

Live Hogs

The 18-day reactivity is the primary indicator; however, trades are made using the 4-day at the expected turning points of the 18-day. The divergence between the midpoint and money flow is dependable for hogs and is a good supporting indicator.

Referring to Figures 5–6 through 5–9, we will now examine each trade point as given by the indicators. At the time of this trading, the contract size on hogs was 30,000 pounds (it has since been increased to 40,000), and the margin was about $700 per contract. We will assume a normal trade of five contracts. Prices are in cents per pound.

Trade Point 1: Day 6   (Long: 5 contracts)

We come into the period holding a long position of five contracts marked-to-market on day 0 at 49.05. Just prior to entering the period the market had made a top which took the 18-day primary indicator over the critical range by a small amount. This signaled holding the long position until the next top in the 4-day "short-cycle" indicator after it had penetrated the zero line. Day six has all the indicators going down as the 4-day turns down from its next top. In addition to a longer divergence (not shown), the M/MF shows a further divergence between days three and five. There was also a divergence between price and the 4-day indicator. Considering the position of the 18-day reactivity and the other factors above, shorting the market on day six is about as close as you will come to a sure thing in commodity trading. Given sufficient margin, this would be a time to sell double your normal position; however, in this case we did not. Price closed near the high on day 6 allowing a sale of 10 contracts at $49.80, offsetting the long and going short.

Trade Point 2: Day 21   (Short: 5 Contracts)

Hog prices decline nicely following day 6, and we first see the 4-day reactivity drop below the critical range on day 12 indicating likely further decline. Based on the previous primary cycle bottom we are expecting a cycle low around day 20, or shortly thereafter. We are looking to buy at the next higher bottom of the 4-day reactivity which may also be expected around day 20.

With the data from day 21 we see a divergence in the M/MF and a possible bottoming in the 18-day reactivity. The 4-day did not make a bottom, just a slight inflection. We buy on day 21 at 47, closing the short and taking a long position. On the short from day six, we get a profit of 2.80, or $840/contract, and a net of $4,075 on the 5-contract trade.

Trade Point 3: Day 25   (Long: 5 Contracts)

With a long position on and prices rising, things are looking good, and as price makes a short-term top at day 23, we're not worried. As the price then reverses, we monitor closely or enter our stop-loss order each day as computed. Prices begin to pull back rather severely and our stop point is hit at 46.35 on day 25. This trade results in a loss of 0.65, $195/contract, for a net loss of $1,100. Since we are still near the expected 36-day cycle bottom, and there are no indications to reverse, we do not sell short.

Referring back to the discussion under trade point two above, one could obviously say that we should have waited for that next higher bottom in the 4-day reactivity. We didn't because of the divergence of the M/MF indicator and the upturn in the 18-day reactivity, our primary indicator. Sufficient strength came into the market to bring our stop-loss point up to limit the loss and that is an OK trade. If the price had not pulled back this far and continued up, we'd be patting ourselves on the back.

Trade Point 4: Day 30   (No Position)

Having been stopped out and at a primary cycle bottom, we are looking for another buy signal. By day 30, we see strong, longer term divergence in the M/MF, we see an upturn from the higher bottom that we were looking for in the 4-day reactivity (also a divergence between this and price), and the 18-day reactivity continues upward. All of this makes for a strong "buy" and we do so at 45.80 and set a stop point at about 20 percent of the average daily range below the low.

As price spikes down again on day 34, but holds above the previous low we could consider adding to the position. Notice how quickly that low price was rejected by the market.

Trade Point 5: Day 44 and 46   (Long: 5 Contracts)

The price climbs sharply and then sets up conditions for a sell trade on day 44. We get a lower top on the 4-day, the 18-day reactivity "appears" to be turning. There has not been a divergence in the M/MF, which works so well with hogs, but the reactivities are the primary indicators. Near the close on day 44 we sell at 47.50 closing the long and going short. The long profit is 1.70, $510 per contract, giving a net of $2425 on five contracts.

The top is re-tested two days later, and a clear divergence is set up on the M/MF indicator, and the 4-day drops further. This is definitely a time to take advantage of the unused margin cushion in the account to add to the position. You could double, but for conservatism we will add three contracts. These are sold at 47.80 on day 46.

Trade Point 6: Day 68   (Short: 8 Contracts)

The price takes a pretty hard hit in the days following day 50, and the 18-day reactivity carries slightly below the lower critical range. This indicates the need for caution here and solid evidence of an upturn before reversing the trade. There is the likelihood that the price will return to near these levels or lower during the next cycle.

A slight rally on day 65 turns the 4-day reactivity and the data point on the 18-day. The smoothed 18-day is still below the critical range, and there are no divergences. The rule is to wait. The price hits the low again on day 67.

On day 68, we see a divergence in the M/MF, and the 18-day reactivity turns up sharply. This is sufficient evidence of a bottom, and we decide to take the short profit and establish a long position. We buy at 44.75 yielding a gross profit of 2.75, or $885 per contract on the original position of five contracts, and 3.05, or $975 per contract, on the added position of three contracts. The total net is $6,870.

Because of the penetration of the lower critical range by the 18-day indicator, it is important to monitor the stop point closely, or to be sure to enter the stop each day to protect against the possible retracement below the entry point. The price comes close to the stop point on days 76 to 78, but it does not go through. As the price recovers and moves higher on day 78 and the 4-day indicator turns up, adding to the position is a definite option.

Trade Point 7: Day 86   (Long: 5 Contracts)

Although the 4-day turns on day 82, the 18-day is considerably above its smoothed line and the detrend of the primary cycle (not shown) showed the cycle bottom close to day 70. Waiting a few days, we find a second down-turn in the 4-day and a crossing of the smoothed line on the 18-day indicator on day 86. Here we reverse the position at 46.80 with a profit of 2.05, $615 per contract, for a total net of $2950.

Live Hog Roundup

We can now summarize these trades and see how things went. Again a round-turn commission of $25 per contract is taken off in determining the net for the full trade. Table 5–2 lists the specifics at each trade and Figure 5–10 shows the net results.

Again, with a relatively conservative approach, handsome profits were made in just 90 trading days. Except for the modest loss in trade two, these positions were never behind the entry point. The maximum margin used was about $5,600 during trade four, giving an inherent annualized rate of return (return on actual margin used) of 480 percent.

5.3 COPPER

The precious metals—gold, silver and platinum—are the most popular with traders in the metals group. In studies of metals to trade, I found platinum to be too volatile for comfort, and gold and silver were both subject to occasional large gaps. Gaps are fine if you are on the right side, but can be devastating if you are not.

Copper is a bit more well behaved and was getting interesting when I was studying the metals in 1987 as it was beginning a major rally. Since that time, copper prices have been high and have made many nice moves for profitable trading.

Copper cycles are relatively irregular, and I have studied and used different trading cycle approaches in the years that I have traded this metal. The short cycle in copper is 6 to 10 days and is somewhat erratic as short cycles tend to be. It is followed with a 4-day reactivity and is used in conjunction with a longer cycle to trigger trades.

The next longer cycle averages about 18 days, but there is rarely an 18-day cycle. The cycles tend to group around 15 days and around 20 days. You can trade this cycle profitably using an 8-day reactivity, but its irregularity is a problem and using a longer cycle is preferable.

The cycle that I have chosen here as primary for trading is a cycle that averages about 32 days with a standard deviation of 5.5. This cycle is normally in the 25- to 36-day range, but don't be too surprised if there is an occasional 20-day or 40-day. Track this cycle with a 14-day reactivity. Make the trades (and add positions) using the 4-day indicator. The 4-day indicator can be a simple momentum, although it is calculated as a reactivity in the following study.

The most consistent cycle has been a relatively long cycle of about six months (~120 trading days). One approach to trading is to trade in the direction of this cycle using a 55-day reactivity and add positions at each turn of the 6- to 10-day cycle using a 4-day momentum. This would have been a profitable approach over the last three years; however, it takes

Table 5–2   Hog Trading Summary

Trade	Buy day # (tp)	Sell	Quan.	Buy @ cents/bu	Sell @	Net ($)
Long	0 (MTM)	6 (1)	5	49.05	49.80	1,125.00
Short	20 (2)	6 (1)	5	47.00	49.80	4,075.00
Long	20 (2)	SO 25 (3)	5	47.00	46.35	(1,100.00)
Long	30 (4)	44 (5)	5	45.80	47.50	2,425.00
Short	—	44 (5)	5	—	47.50	
	68 (6)	46 (5)	+3	44.75	47.80	6,670.00
Long	68 (6)	86 (7)	5	44.75	46.80	2,950.00
Short	90 (MTM)	86 (7)	5	47.22	46.80	505.00
			TOTAL			$16,650.00

*Notes: (tp)—Trade point number; MTM—Marked to market; SO—Stopped out; Commission is $25 / contract round turn (not taken on incoming position, but is taken on out-going position).

Figure 5–10   Trading Profits—Live Hogs

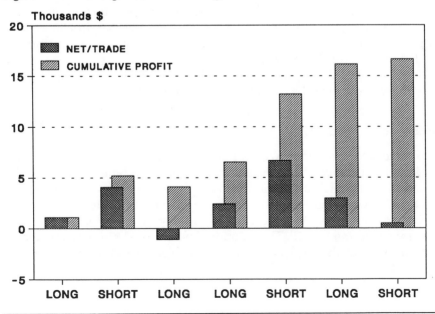

considerable margin, sometimes more draw-down, and of course, a great deal of patience and discipline.

Figure 5–11 shows the futures price and the stop-loss band for copper during the first 90 days of 1989. The price was volatile during this period and offered good trading opportunities. You can also see that the price behavior falls into the 25- to 36-day cycle range mentioned above. We will track this cycle using a 14-day reactivity shown in Figure 5–12.

The primary indicator for trading copper is the 14-day reactivity. Use the 4-day momentum (Figure 5–13) as the short-cycle indicator; however, caution must be exercised in the use of this indicator. As you study the graphs, you will see that the 4-day indicator generally gives a first warning of the upcoming trade point at its first turn. The best trade point then is most often the second turn in this short-term indicator. This is because there are usually three cycles of shorter duration that make up the trading cycle. These can be quite irregular, but they can be used.

Copper could be traded quite successfully during this period using only the 14-day indicator. As you follow through the trade points, you will find this to be true. Overall, I have found that the performance can be improved by adding to the position on the second of the short cycles. This addition then makes use of profit margin already added by the first trade. So the trading scheme is to make the primary trade, i.e., close previous trade and take initial position, on the turn in the 14-day reactivity (generally the second turn in the 4-day) and add on the next turn in the 4-day. The number of contracts, of course, depends on the margin allocated to copper. For the examples here the trade is two contracts, and a third is added using the 4-day indicator.

The M/MF divergence (Figure 5–14) worked well as a supplementary indicator during the period of this demonstration.

Trade Point 1: Day 17   (Long: 3 Contracts)

We came into this period with a long position, so the first point we are looking for is the place to close the long position and initiate a short. The 4-day indicator makes its first turn sharply on day 12 while the 14-day flattens. The 4-day goes up slightly on day 16 and turns down on day 17. This is accompanied by a turn in the 14-day, and by the setting of a divergence in the M/MF. This is trade day and five contracts are sold at 129.10 to offset the long position and establish the initial short of two contracts.

Figure 5-11 Copper Futures Price

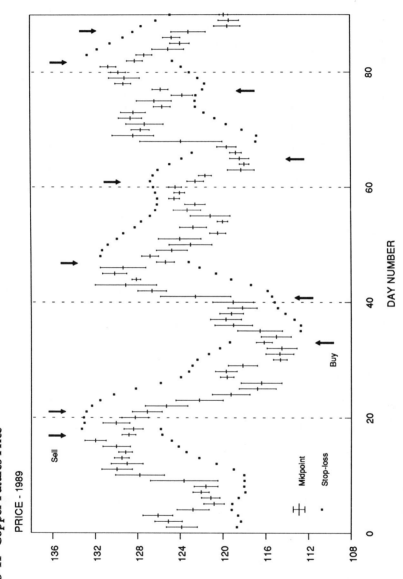

PRICE - 1989

Figure 5-12 14-Day Reactivity—Copper

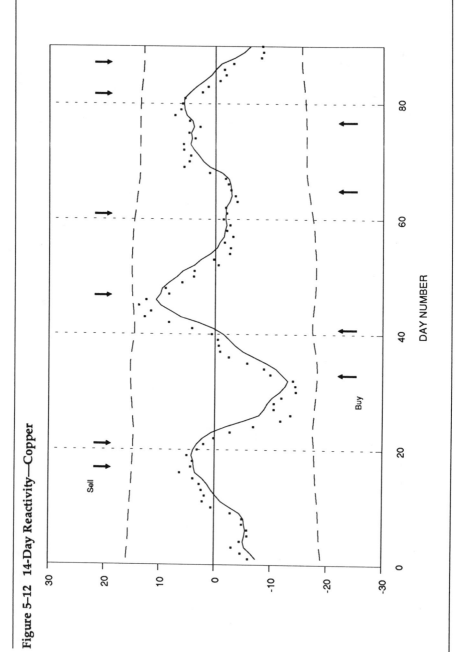

Figure 5-13 4-Day Momentum—Copper

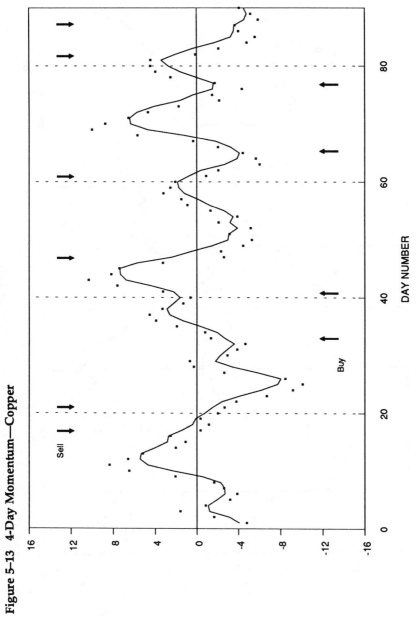

Figure 5–14 Midpoint and Money Flow

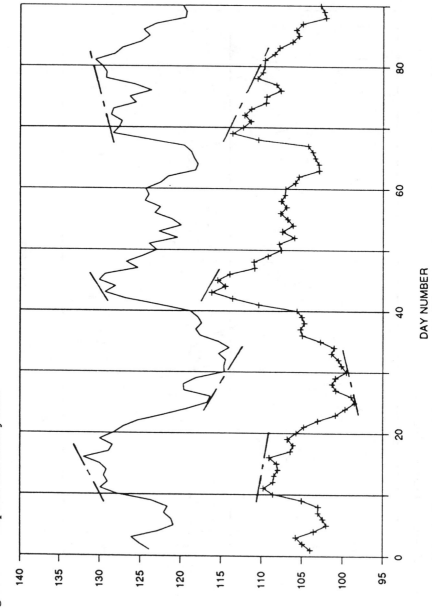

DAY NUMBER

The 4-day makes another little up and then down on day 20 accompanied by the definite turn in the 14-day as the data crosses the exponential average smoothing line. This is where we add to the short position and get that off at 127.60. Selling the two contracts on day 17 and one on day 20 gives a short of three at an average price of 128.60.

Trade Point 2: Day 33 and 41   (Short: 3 Contracts)

The 4-day indicator makes its clear second turn on day 33 and is accompanied by the clear turn in the 14-day and the confirming divergence in the M/MF so there is not much doubt about this one. Closing the short and going long late in the day gets us the trade at 115.80. This makes an average gross profit of 12.80, $3,200 per contract on the short trade for a net after commissions of $9,525.

This trade isn't over yet. The 4-day pulls back and turns up again on day 41. This is still early in the primary cycle and one contract is added to the long position at 123.10, giving an average price on the three contracts of 118.23.

Trade Point 3: Day 47 and 60   (Long: 3 Contracts)

The price spikes up in the following couple of days and turns down on day 44 causing the first turn in the 4-day. The price recovers, makes a second top and starts down. This makes only a small jog in the 4-day, but turns the 14-day through its smoothing line. This, confirmed by the short-term divergence in the M/MF says this (day 47) is the trade day. We missed the top by a few points, but that's the way this game goes. The trade goes off at 125.20. This is an average of 6.97 on the price and a net on the three long contracts of $5,150.

The second turn in the 4-day comes on day 60 and we sell the third contract at 124.60, now giving us a 3-contract short position at an average selling price of 125.00.

Trade Point 4: Day 65 and 77   (Short: 3 Contracts)

The up-turn in the 4-day and the 14-day comes on day 65, where we buy the market at 118.20. You will notice that there is not a confirming divergence in the M/MF, but the turn in both the primary and trading indicator right at the average cycle length point is certainly sufficient. Remember that the M/MF is supporting only and isn't necessary to the trade. Its primary purpose is to give you psychological support in your trade; you will be more comfortable with its confirmation. In this case, you may want to watch the trade a little more closely and, indeed, things are a little choppy.

Having closed the short at 118.20, that trade yielded an average of 6.80 for a total net gain $5,025.

Prices react sharply to the upside, and then things get a little murky around days 74, 75 and 76 after the first turn in the 4-day, and the direction of the 14-day is definitely in question. There would be a definite tendency to close the long trade on day 76 except for two solid reasons. We are only 10 days into this cycle, and the 4-day indicator shows the short cycle to be at an expected bottom. That doesn't mean that the high has not been made, but it means there is a good chance for a recovery. If the price had gone below the stop line, the long position should have been closed, and you wait and see what happens next.

In either case, getting out because of the indicators on day 76 or if the stop line had been penetrated, the right move would be to buy back in as both indicators turn up again on day 77. This would be psychologically difficult but necessary. Having remained with the position, we use the upturn on day 77 to add to the long position at 125.90.

Trade Point 5: Day 82 and 87   (Long: 3 Contracts)

The 4-day and the 14-day turn down on day 82 and we sell at 128.30. This gives a gain on the long position of 7.53, and a net of $5,575. An additional contract is sold on day 87 at 122.20 for an average short position price of 126.20. This last trade is market-to-market at 119.60 on day 90 for a net of $5,200. Were we continuing, this trade would eventually be closed on day 101 at 109 for a gross profit of 17.20 yielding a net of $12,825.

Copper Summary

Obviously, following the system with courage, discipline and patience paid off handsomely during this time period. The specifics of the trades are given in Table 5-3. When reading these tables, remember that QUAN is the number of contracts entered, and that all of these are always offset at the next trade point in the opposite direction. For example, when "2" and "+1" are bought, obviously 3 are sold at the following sell point. The results are summarized in Figure 5-15.

There are a couple of other points worth noting. You will notice that if the 4-day indicator were discarded and the trades made only with the

Table 5–3   Copper Trade Summary

Trade	Buy	Sell	Quan.	Buy @	Sell @	Net
	Day # (tp)			cents/bu		($)
Long	0 (MTM)	17 (1)	3	122.25	129.10	5,137.50
Short	—	10 (1)	2	—	129.10	
	33 (2)	20 (1)	+1	115.80	127.60	9,525.00
Long	33 (2)	—	2	115.80	—	
	41 (2)	47 (3)	+1	123.10	125.20	5,150.00
Short	—	47 (3)	2	—	125.20	
	65 (4)	60 (3)	+1	118.20	124.60	5,025.00
Long	65 (4)	—	2	118.20	—	
	77 (4)	82 (5)	+1	125.90	128.30	5,575.00
Short	—	32 (5)	2	—	128.30	
	90 (MTM)	88 (5)	+1	119.60	123.30	5.200.00
			TOTAL			$35,612.50

*Notes: (tp)—Trade point number; MTM—Marked to market; SO—Stopped out; Commission is $25 / contract round turn (not taken on incoming position, but is taken on out-going position).

Figure 5-15   Trading Profits—Copper

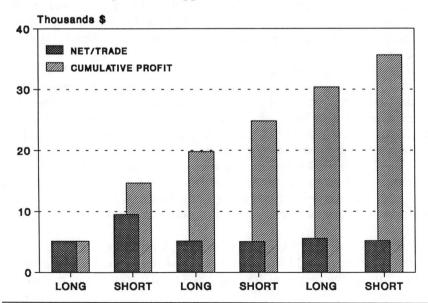

14-day, the profit would still be considerable. Use of the 4-day is most useful in adding the additional contract after the first trade.

At the time of these trades, the margin requirement at my broker was $1,600 per contract. You will see that the third contract added was partly covered, or more than fully covered by the trade equity on the original position. For the five trades there was open trade equity of $750, $3,650, $300, $3,800 and $3,050 respectively at the time the third contract was added. The contribution to the total profit over the period made by the added contract was about $6,500.

5.4 COTTON

Cotton is a challenge to trade. The margin is relatively low, the prices sometimes erratic, and there can be substantial moves. As with most things, the greater the potential, the greater the risk.

The price behavior of cotton for the prior four years breaks down into four cycles of roughly 10, 20, 40, and 80 trading days, however these cycles are not consistent and are not necessarily multiples of one another. The actual mean values are 11, 21, 41, and 75. The standard deviations are 20, 25, 18, and 12 percent respectively.

The 75-day cycle is the most consistent but is a little long for my style of trading. The principal disadvantage of this cycle is that the amplitude is not appreciably greater than that of the 40-day cycle, so good trading opportunities can be missed and you will find yourself sitting through troughs where big gains go nearly to zero and back. Not comfortable trading.

The 40-day cycle is regular enough and can be traded with an 18-day reactivity. You have to watch carefully since this cycle can sometimes be 30 days and occasionally 50 days. It is helpful to maintain a 35- or 40-day momentum as a guide to the longer cycle direction when trading the 40-day cycle. Use a 5- or 6-day reactivity as the trading indicator to time trade points and to add to the position.

The cotton market was in a fairly sustained rally for the first 90 days of 1989. The price behavior is shown in Figure 5–16 and the primary indicator; the 18-day reactivity is shown in Figure 5–17. Figures 5–18 and 5–19 show the 6-day reactivity trading indicator and the M/MF respectively.

The cotton contract is 50,000 pounds making a 1 cent/lb move worth $500. Prices are quoted in cents and hundredths of a cent. The margin on cotton during the period of trading was $1,500/contract and the normal

Figure 5–16   Cotton Futures Price

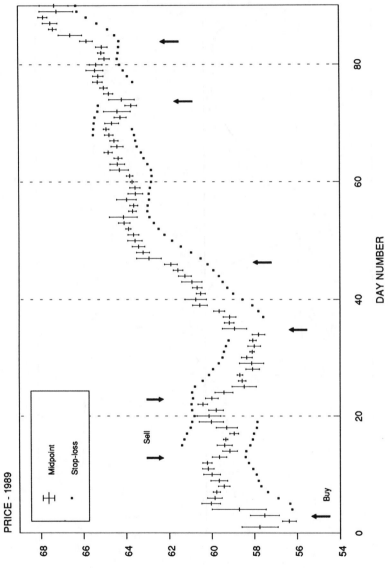

PRICE - 1989

Figure 5-17 18-Day Reactivity—Cotton

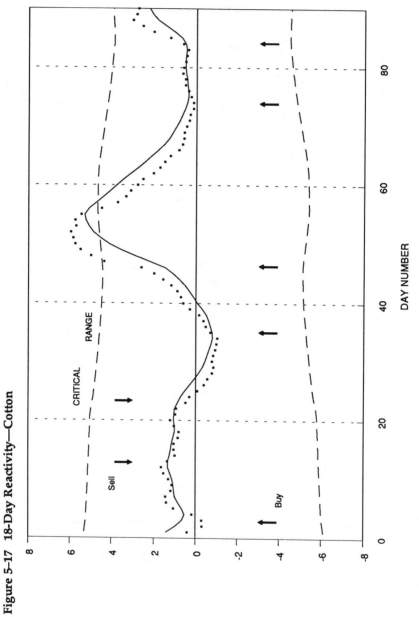

Figure 5-18 6-Day Reactivity—Cotton

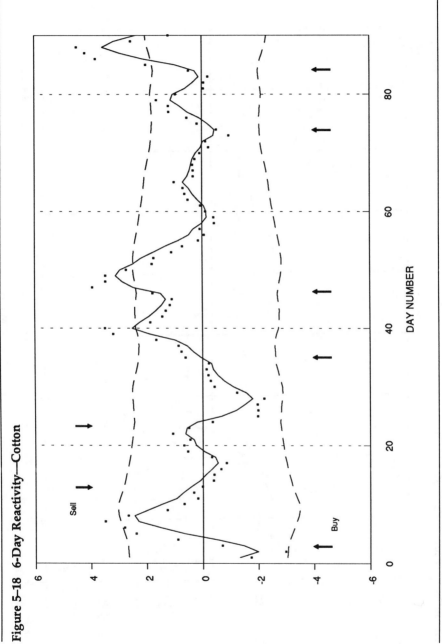

Figure 5-19 Midpoint and Money Flow

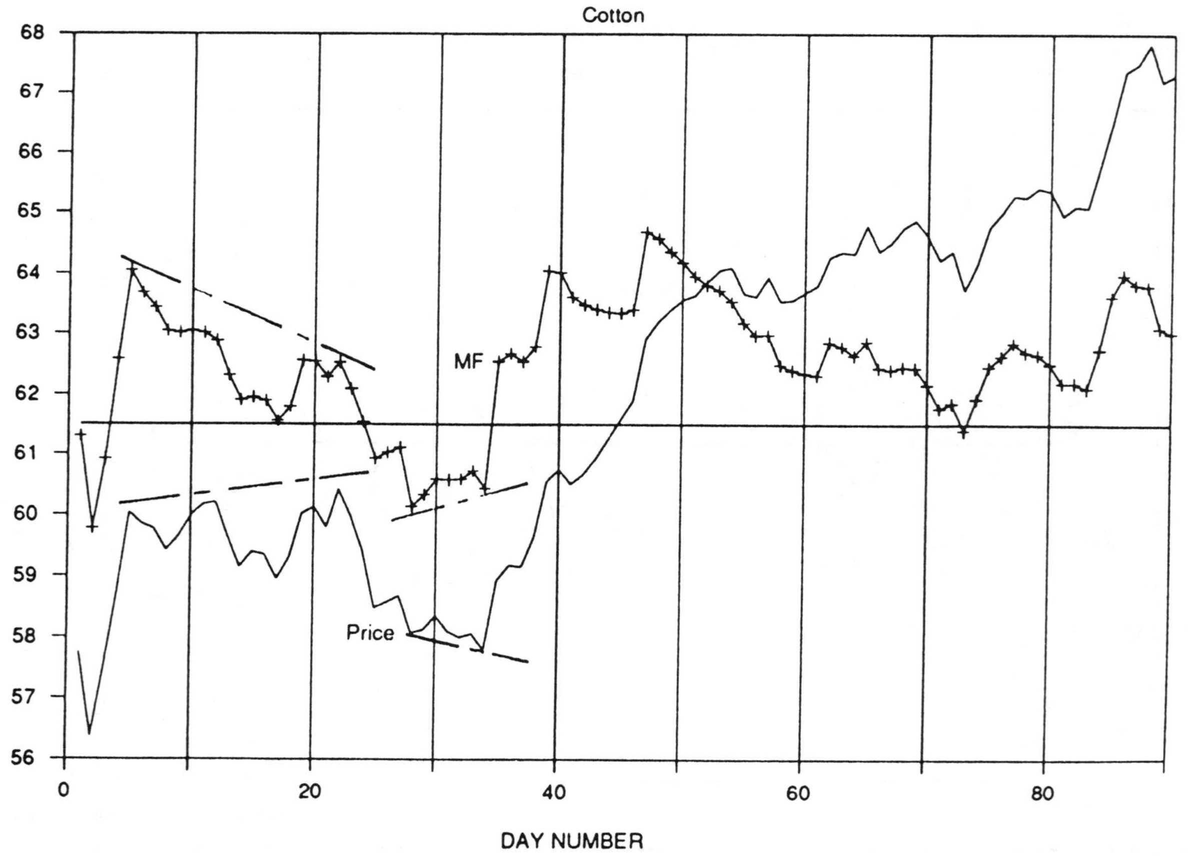

trade will be two contracts on the initial trade with an add-on of one contract.

Trade Point 1: Day 3   (Long: 2 Contracts)

The buy signal for the cycle coming into this period occurred a few days prior to the period shown. The downward spike into day two retraced most of the move to that point. The add-on trade is made at the point where the short-cycle indicator, the 6-day reactivity, (Figure 5–18) turns up on day 3. This is the second up-turn in the 6-day reactivity, and as was the case with copper, the second turn in the trading indicator many times provides the best trade point. We add one contract at 57.80.

Trade Point 2: Day 13 and 23   (Long: 3 Contracts)

In the period from day 5 to day 20, things are not very clear. The 6-day traces the short cycle clearly but the 18-day is vacillating. My analysis goes like this. I ignore the turn in both the 6-day and the 18-day at days 7 and 8 because it is too early in the cycle, it is the first top in the 6-day, there is no divergence in the M/MF, price is considerably above the stop point, and the strong run-up is likely to be followed by some continued strength. Enough reasons to stand pat.

But the downturn of the 18-day on day 13 causes a re-evaluation. The 6-day has done a little jog, and the M/MF has formed a divergence. Another factor that is not shown here is the 35-day momentum and detrend of the 75-day cycle shows the long cycle going down toward a bottom. There is no choice but to exit the long and go short on day 13. The trade goes off at 59.40. We pick up an average of 1.2 points on the three contract long position which nets $1,725.

The rally on days 18 and 19 causes concern but it does not hit the stop point. Also note the divergent tops on all three indicators. By day 22 it is obvious that here is an opportunity to add to the short, but we don't actually do it until day 23 when all indicators turn down. Already short two contracts, we add one more at 59.85. The short position is now three contracts sold at an average price of 59.55.

Trade Point 3: Day 35 and 46   (Short: 3 Contracts)

The 6-day turns up on day 29, giving the "get ready" signal. The primary indicator turns up on day 35 along with resumed upward movement in the 6-day and the formation of a divergence in the M/MF. We exit the short and go long. The jump upward on day 35 makes for a disappointing trade point and the trade goes at 58.85. The profit on the short totals 0.70 points, and the net profit on the three contracts is $975.

The strong rally is accompanied by the next upturn in the 10-day cycle as signaled on day 46. Add one contract at 62.07.

Trade Point 4: Day 66   (Long: 3 Contracts)

As this primary cycle tops just after day 50, we see that the 18-day reactivity goes above the critical line. The rules require holding the position at least until the next top in the short-cycle indicator. This occurs on day 65, and we notice that the data points on the 18-day reactivity have exceeded the critical range by just under 40 percent. This is an indication for neither a reversal nor a hold, but for closing the long position and waiting for the next buy signal to go long again.

For a moderate excursion beyond the critical range, as is the case here, it is prudent to close the position, but not reverse, and wait for a signal to re-establish the position. For a large excursion beyond the critical line, for example, a smoothed reactivity value of 1.5 times the critical value, or more, definitely hold the position and add (double) at the next trade signal. Maintain the protection of the stop-loss.

Another point to be made here is that divergences in the M/MF after the primary indicator significantly exceeds the critical range usually are not meaningful.

In this case, you could have made a bit more profit and saved commission by holding the position, but you most assuredly would have paid a price of discomfort with your large profit sitting there vulnerable. In any case, we close the long, not at the turn in the primary indicator, but at the next lower top in the short-cycle indicator. This occurs on day 66, and we make the trade at 64.30 for an average gain of 4.38 points and a net on three contracts of $6,490.

Had there been a significant penetration of the zero line (more than 25 percent of the critical range) by the 6-day reactivity at days 58 to 60 could have indicated reversing the position on day 66.

Trade Point 5: Day 74 and 84   (No position)

The primary indicator turns up again without penetrating zero indicating continued upward pressure. We re-institute our long position as both indicators turn up again on day 74 at 65.05. The 40-day cycle is operating nicely. We add to the position on the next turn in the 6-day on day 84 at 65.83, giving the 3 contracts an average price of 65.31.

This trade is marked-to-market on day 90 at 66.94. Following day 90, the 18-day tops below the critical line and the 6-day makes its next lower top and turns down on day 99. The long could be closed at 68.47.

Cotton Summary

The cotton trades are given in table 5.4. The initial entry in each trade is two contracts and the additional entry is one contract. There are four trades for the period, the results of which are summarized in Figure 5–20.

Based on the most recent three years of data, I've adjusted the cycle structure used for trading cotton. During 1990 and 1991, I found that a primary cycle averaging about 34 days was reliable and was traded with a 16-day reactivity. A 5-day reactivity works well as a trading indicator.

5.5 EURODOLLARS

There are two things about trading Eurodollars that will make the demonstration trading different from the commodities previously discussed. The first is that the trading strategy uses two different cycle length indicators as primary indicators at different times, and second, the trading strategy is longer term, so it is necessary to look at a period of more than 90 days to give a proper example.

Eurodollar prices tend to follow longer term trends and the cycle that I have found to be most useful for trading has a period of about six months. The shorter cycles of interest are about 10 days, 30 days, and 60 days. The 10-day cycle is useful for fine tuning the timing of trades and for adding positions. The 30-day cycle becomes the primary cycle at the bottoms of the 6-month cycle and, although quite variable in length overall, it is quite regular in its occurrence at longer cycle bottoms. The 60-day cycle is not used directly in the trading, however I track it and use it as secondary information. It has value in that it will usually show a divergence with the price and the long-term indicator at major trend changes.

The indicators in use during this period are a 4-day, 13-day, 26-day, and 60-day. The primary long-term indicator is a simple 60-day momentum. After 100 days from the last long-term cycle bottom, the 13-day reactivity becomes the primary indicator for two cycles. This gets us through the long-term cycle bottom, and we again revert to the 60-day indicator. Because of the irregularities in the 30-day cycle, it can be risky

Table 5–4   Cotton Trade Summary

Trade	Buy	Sell	Quan.	Buy @	Sell @	Net
	day # (tp)			cents/bu		($)
Long	0 (MTM)	—	2	58.40	—	
	3 (1)	13 (2)	+1	57.80	59.40	1,725.00
Short		13 (2)	2		59.40	
	35 (3)	23 (2)	+1	58.85	59.85	975.00
Long	35 (3)	—	2	58.85	—	
	46 (3)	66 (4)	+1	62.07	64.30	6,490.00
Long	74 (5)	—	2	65.00	—	
	85 (5)	90 (MTM)	+1	65.83	66.94	2.420.00
			TOTAL			$11,610.00

*Notes: (tp)—Trade point number; MTM—Marked to market; SO—Stopped out; Commission is $25 / contract round turn (not taken on incoming position, but is taken on out-going position).

Figure 5–20   Trading Profits—Cotton

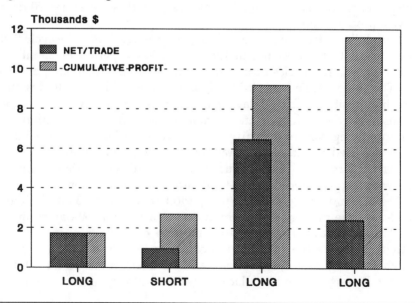

to add to the position during the times when we are trading this cycle, and that will not be done here.

It's confusing at first, but it makes sense after you follow it for awhile. In simple terms, it is necessary to do this because the price becomes more volatile at the extremes of the longer term cycle. This is common for most commodities. I have found (so far at least) that for Eurodollars the cycle tops are well enough behaved to stick with the longer term indicator as primary, but at the bottoms some large and profitable shorter term fluctuations take place.

Using this strategy over the period from January 1988 to March 1991, resulted in 22 of 29 trades being profitable (76 percent) with the average winning trade being over 10 times larger than the losing trades.

Each contract controls $250,000 worth of Eurodollars, and prices are quoted in cents/$ (or percent and hundredths of a percent). A full point move is worth $2,500 per contract. The margin requirement during the period was $700/contract, so the normal position for this study is five contracts. Adding to a position will be done in increments of two contracts.

Again, we will start at the beginning of 1989, but this time we will look at a 180-day period. And this particular period was pretty wild in the Eurodollar market with some large price changes taking place. The price behavior is shown in Figure 5–21. Figure 5–22 shows the 60-day momentum and the detrend of the 130-day cycle.

The last long-term cycle low was 100 days prior to the start of the trading period shown. What is seen in this period is a major trend change from a long-term bear market to a bull market. The prior 6-month cycle top occurred before the mid cycle point, and we see here that the top occurs late in the cycle. The primary cycle here was somewhat extended with the bottom at about day 60 giving a period length of about 160 days.

Trade Point 1: Day 8   (Short: 9 Contracts)

Now looking at the actual trading strategy, we will first note that coming into this period we are already 100 days into this primary cycle, and the strategy is to look at the 13-day reactivity as the primary trade indicator. This indicator is shown in Figure 5–23. Since we are going to verify the trade and add positions with the 4-day indicator we need to take a look at that also (Figure 5–24).

We see that on days 4 and 5, both the 4- and 13-day indicators turn up as the down-trend stalls out. However, for reversing a position on a longer term cycle trend, I want to see a definite indication that the 13-day

Figure 5–21 Eurodollar Futures Price

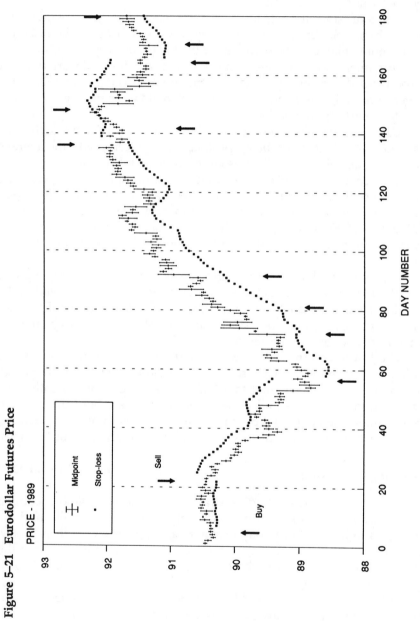

Figure 5-22 Long-Term Cycles—Euros

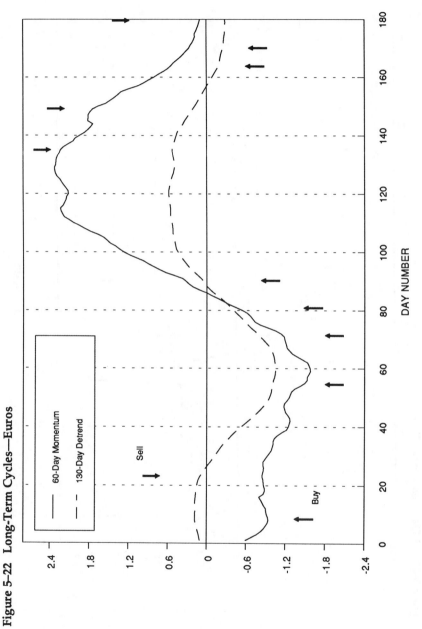

Figure 5-23 13-Day Reactivity—Euros

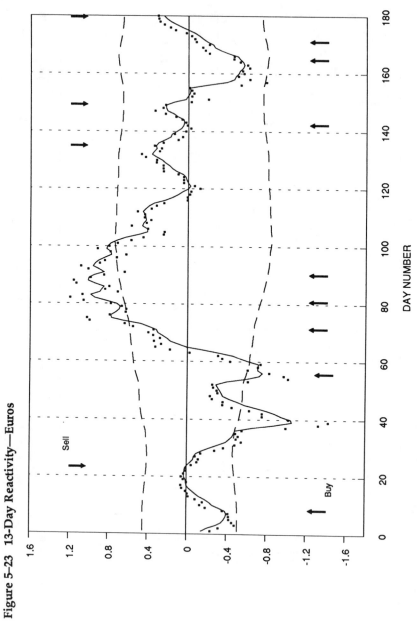

Figure 5-24 4-Day Momentum—Euros

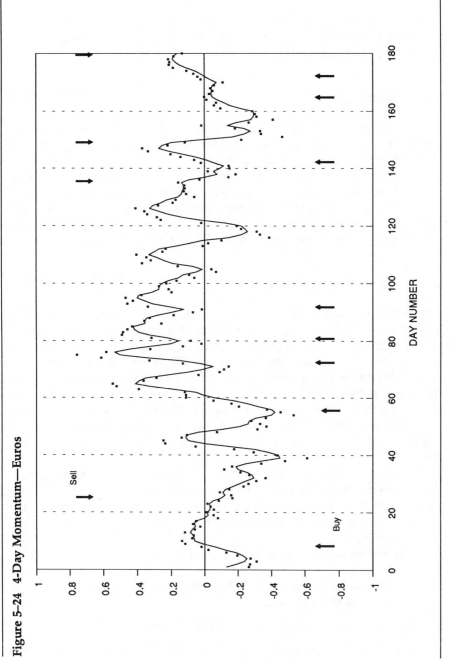

is crossing its 0.33 smoothed average. This doesn't happen until day eight. Eurodollars are bought at 90.40 to close the short and take a standard long position of five contracts.

Trade Point 2: Day 23   (Long: 5 Contracts)

In the next couple of weeks, the price is unable to rally, and the 13-day reactivity gives a sell signal on day 23. Trading late in the day gets the trade off at 90.44 as we sell ten contracts to offset the long position of five contracts and go short five contracts. The long trade gained 0.04 points to yield a modest gross profit of $500, which nets $375 after commissions.

In this case, trading the 13-day indicator coming into the bottom of the 6-month cycle was not advantageous. However, over the period from 1987 through 1990, experience has shown that it was the best approach.

Trade Point 3: Day 56, 72, 81   (Short: 5 Contracts)

Proceeding forward a day at a time, we see that on day 32, the 4-day indicator turns and the 13-day indicates a possible turn. Since this is where a bottom of the roughly 30-day cycle is expected, there is a great temptation to buy before the 13-day actually crosses its smoothed line. Don't fall into the trap of anticipating tops or bottoms just because it is in the proper window. We wait for the 13-day to cross, and the price declines sharply further in the next week taking the 13-day beyond the critical line by about a factor of three. This is a clear indication to hold the short position and wait for lower prices while the indicator makes a higher bottom.

We are in a specific situation here that needs study and judgment. Price bottoms on day 54, and on day 56 we have buy signals on the 4- and 13-day indicators. But there are some things to worry about. The 13-day did not penetrate through zero, and we have a cycle of only about 20 days. Is it time to buy?

The factors mitigating in favor of buying are these:

1. At this point, we are 157 days from the last primary cycle bottom—at the high end.

2. It is at the point of an expected 50-60 day cycle bottom.

3. There is a strong divergence of both the 4-day and the 13-day indicators with the price.

4. The 60-day momentum (Figure 5.22) did not reach any extreme negative value which would have indicated a strong continuing down trend.

What occurred here was the final "blow-off" of a long-term down trend. This is, in fact, the formation of one of the chart people's favorite formations, the head and shoulders. It is not uncommon to find that a longer term bottom will bisect a shorter cycle giving this formation and a buy indication at a shortened or lengthened cycle. The price-indicator divergence is almost always operative in these cases.

On day 56, we reverse the position and monitor carefully until any doubts we may have are overcome. The buy is made at 88.98 for a gain of 1.46 and a net profit of $18,250 on the five-contract short position.

There is more buying to be done here. Price moves up strongly through day 66 and then makes a small correction. As the 4-day turns up again on day 72, we add two contracts to our position at 89.54. By day 75, the 13-day has gone significantly past the critical range and we have another buy signal from the 4-day on day 81, and add two more contracts at 90.31. As the strong up-trend continues into our long-term cycle top, we add two more contracts on day 92 at 91.15. Additional positions could be added on day 106 and on day 119. I hesitate to do so because the risk gets greater as you near the top of the long-term cycle and some high volatility that usually occurs at such tops can make you very uncomfortable. For this study, we will stay with our total of 11 contracts purchased at an average price of 89.72.

Trade Point 4: Day 136   (Long: 11 Contracts)

The sell signal we are waiting for as the 60-day momentum makes its top is a lower top on the 13-day reactivity, **after** it has penetrated the zero line. Around day 120 the 13-day goes just slightly past the zero line. So when the 4-day and the 13-day break to the downside along with the price on day 136, it may not seem clear what to do.

The 60-day indicator is coming off a second top and the 4-day made a significant penetration of the zero line around day 120. Reviewing all the conditions and the timing, most factors indicate to sell. The question of the 13-day reactivity going only slightly through zero is neutral, certainly not contradictory to the other information. With the sizable profit in place, prudence says to sell. The position is closed at 91.83 and we institute a short position of five contracts. The profit on the long position is 2.11 giving a net on the 11 contracts of $57,800.

This is the kind of move and trade that makes this business attractive. They don't come frequently in any one commodity, but if you are trading five or six different commodities you ought to get in on at least one of these every year.

Trade Point 5: Day 142   (Short: 5 Contracts)

Generally, in any market following a long, strong move such as has occurred here, the top (or bottom) will get "tested" at least once and perhaps more than once. We can expect that here. On day 142, the price begins to rally again. The 13-day has still not gone significantly below zero and turns up along with the 4-day. It is best to exit the short and wait to reinstitute the position as the indicators turn down again. We get out with a small loss at 91.85 and, of course, commissions of $125.

Trade Point 6: Day 148   (No position)

The sell signal comes again on day 148. At this point in the cycle, the odds are obviously greater for this to be a good sell-off and selling the normal position of five contracts plus an add-on of two contracts would be justified. For a more conservative approach here, we will just sell 5 at 92.12.

Trade Point 7: Day 164 and 171   (Short: 5 Contracts)

On day 155, the price makes one more stab at testing the high and immediately sells off rather sharply. Since it is at this point more than 100 days into the 6-month cycle we are watching for the turn of the 13-day reactivity and will trade the roughly 30-day cycle for two cycles. The upturn comes on day 164 and the buy is at 91.44. The close of the short position gives a net profit of $8,375.

The price remains flat and the 4-day makes a divergent higher bottom on day 171 giving a good indication to add to the position. Two contracts are added, again at 91.44, for a long position of seven contracts.

Trade Point 8: Day 180   (Long: 7 Contracts)

The next trade comes just at the end of the period. We see the 4-day indicator turn on day 179 with the 13-day following on day 180. The long position is closed at 91.73 for a net of $4,900.

Eurodollar Summary

Table 5-5 lists the trades made for the first 180 days of 1989. The initial position for each trade is five contracts with each added position being two contracts. The round-turn commission is taken as $25 per contract. The trading results are summarized in Figure 5-25.

5.6 BEWARE, THE TRAP!

One of the things to notice in the foregoing trading examples is that when things went wrong and the stop point was hit the trade was closed, no questions asked. It was stressed in Chapter 4 that one of the most important tasks of the trader is to make sure that losses are limited to those allowed within the system. Because of the importance of this aspect, we're going to look at an example of a real trading situation where an otherwise experienced and successful fictitious trader got into the loss trap. And "trap" is the appropriate word because it is something that springs suddenly upon the unsuspecting person; which means that you may not realize that you're in it until it is too late.

Ralph Trader had trades going in hogs, wheat, copper and cotton. The trades were going well, as had the previous half dozen trades. He was well ahead on the month and the previous evening he had brought the accounting spreadsheet up to date and found that the current months profits had far eclipsed the previous months modest loss, and it felt good to know that things were on track. When his friend called, Ralph mentioned how pleased he was with the way the trading was going.

The previous four out of five trades on copper had been profitable and Ralph's confidence in trading copper was high. The copper trade that he had on now was a short position in the September contract. It's day number 160 and the trade was ahead. Let's look at the graphs for copper in Figures 5-26 through 5-29 and see what had transpired in the recent past.

Looking at Figure 5–26, we see prices coming down steeply into this period and Ralph had a short position working which produced substantial profit. This was reversed on day 107, and the long position had worked into another profit.

Ralph generally didn't pay attention to other opinions about commodity price behavior, but he had happened to see an article in *The Wall Street Journal* where a trader for some large firm was quoted as predicting continued downward pressure on copper prices; predicting a price in the "eighties" by September. The rally between days 105 and 120 was clearly

Table 5–5   Eurodollar Trade Summary

Trade	Buy day # (tp)	Sell day # (tp)	Quan.	Buy @ cents/bu	Sell @ cents/bu	Net ($)
Short	8 (1)	0 (MTM)	9	90.40	90.62	2,750.00
Long	8 (1)	23 (2)	5	90.40	90.44	375.00
Short	56 (3)	23 (2)	5	88.98	90.44	18,125.00
Long	56 (3)	—	5	88.98	—	
	72 (3)	—	+2	89.54	—	
	81 (3)	—	+2	90.31	—	
	92 (3)	136 (4)	+2	91.15	91.83	56,800.00
Short	142 (5)	136 (4)	5	91.85	91.83	(375.00)
Short	164 (7)	148 (6)	5	91.44	92.12	8,375.00
Long	164 (7)	—	5	91.44	—	
	171 (7)	180 (8)	+2	91.44	91.73	4,900.00
					Total	$90,950.00

*Notes: (tp)—Trade point number; MTM—Marked to market; SO—Stopped out; Commission is $25 / contract round turn (not taken on incoming position, but is taken on out-going position).

Figure 5–25   Trading Profits—Eurodollars

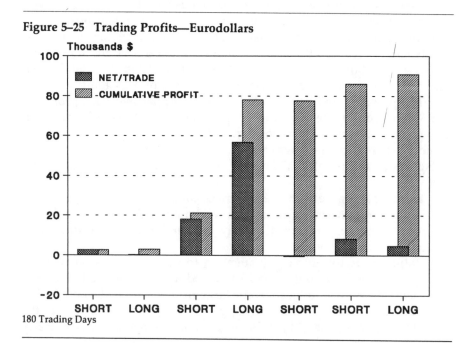

Figure 5–26 September Copper, 1991—Getting Trapped

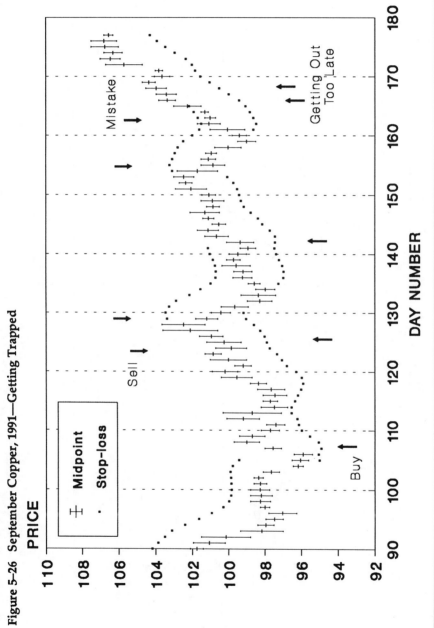

Figure 5-27 14-Day Reactivity, September Copper

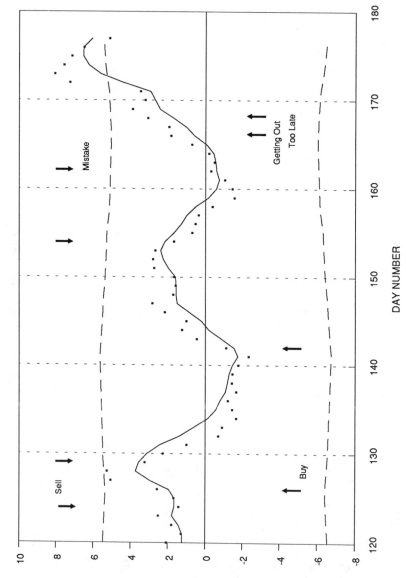

Figure 5-28 4-Day Reactivity, September Copper

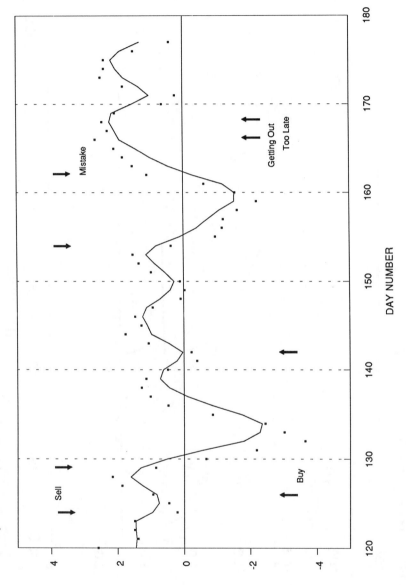

Figure 5-29 Price and Money Flow

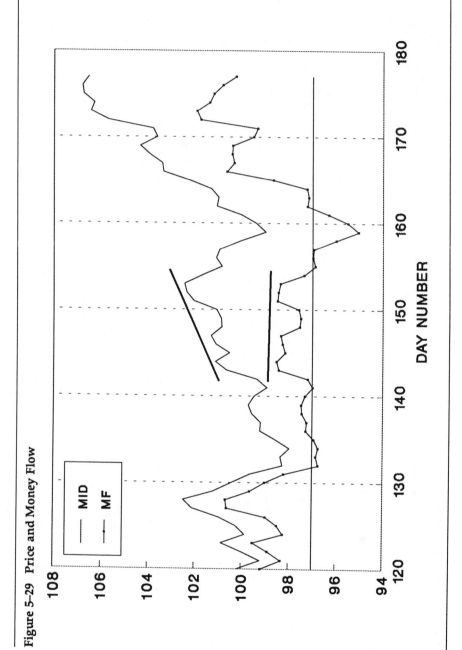

weak, and the long position was reversed on day 124 as both the 4-day and 14-day reversed (Figures 5–27 and 5–28). This position was closed at a slight loss on day 126 when prices rallied again, and the indicators turned up. But then on day 129, the short was put on again, and the price subsequently went down.

This short position was closed at a profit on day 143 and a long position put on. This cycle had been shorter than the previous one, but the detrend showed about 32 days, so that was fine. Again the long position was working at a profit up through day 150. Somewhere during this time Ralph happened to catch part of an interview on CNBC/FNN in which an "expert" was asked what he thought about copper now that the economy was on the upturn. He opined that there was abundant supply and that he thought copper would be a good buy down around 95, basically a re-test of the low a few weeks earlier.

Ralph sold copper on day 154 as both the 4-day short-cycle indicator and the 14-day primary indicator turned down. At this point there was also an apparent divergence between the midpoint and money flow indicator (Figure 5–29) between this and the last top. This looked like the setup for another good sell-off and, indeed, through day 159 the price dropped sharply. So things really did look good as Ralph reviewed the accounting and talked to his friend.

But then on day 161, the price rallied for the second day and had come up sharply. The 4-day had clearly turned, and the 14-day was looking like a turn. Could this be time to reverse the position? Probably not, because it was only about 26 days from the last bottom; a little too short, particularly since the cycle which had bottomed after the steep sell-off into day 105 had been 42 days. And for weeks the behavior had looked weak, and the experts had predicted weakness. It must be just a short-term retracement. Best to stay with the short position and watch the stop point closely. Ralph had not actually put any stop orders into the market for some time now; he felt it wasn't really necessary as long as he was monitoring the market activity and things were working well.

Shortly after the opening on day 162, the price had gone through the stop point by a quarter of a point and then sold off. This had to be the top. He made the decision to get out if the high was taken out, otherwise, even though the indicators were now both indicating "buy," he would stay with the short position and reap the benefits of guts and patience. And, indeed, the high held, and for the next two days the highs were lower as the price traded in a small range.

Remember as you look at this that in the actual situation you don't have the benefit of looking ahead. The best way to visualize this situation is to cover the graph from the day in question forward, and try to understand how this unfolds. Chances are that if you trade, you will experience a similar situation.

On day 164, Ralph Trader is uneasy about this copper behavior. It is still showing some strength but hasn't gone through the stop or taken out the high of day 162. Also, now looking at the 4-day indicator he sees that it is five days into what is usually an eight- to ten-day cycle. This reinforces the belief that this is a corrective move and that the primary cycle bottom will come at the bottom of the next short cycle. This seems like a great opportunity to add to the short position, and he does this at 101.20. He shut out the secondary fact that the longer term 110- to 120-day cycle has apparently bottomed around day 115.

On day 165, the quotes shortly after the opening brings the frightening news that the price has gapped to the upside with a high of 102.40 and a low of 101.80. Oh my! This makes no sense! Now what? Well, best to watch closely and if the gap is closed, stay with the short position because now the profit has turned to a loss, and according to the "opening gap" day trade rules that he used to do, if the price closes the gap and goes just below the previous day's high, then it is likely to close below the gap point. If the price takes out the high so far, then the trade will have to be closed. He turns attention to his other trades, checks the quote again, and goes for a short break to relieve some stress.

Now we can see that Ralph is clearly confused. He is still convinced that the price is going lower. The experts aren't going to be buying back in until down around 95, right? But by now three rules are being broken. First, both the primary and the trading indicator are clearly going against the position and indicate that the trade should be on the long side; second, the stop-loss point has now clearly been bypassed; and, third, the rule says that on an opening gap against the position, the position should be closed and possibly re-entered on the opening gap rule, but only if the indicators are not being violated. But the preconceived notion of lower prices and the inability to accept the loss leads him to focus on finding reasons to justify continuing the trade. The two main factors are that the cycle length seems too short for the bottom to be in, and the trading cycle should be expected to be making a top here, so a sell-off must be eminent.

Upon returning from his break, Ralph has realized that the copper trade is in trouble, and it is now a matter of how to best extricate himself from this situation. But rather than just close it, he waits; and the consequence is that suddenly the price rallies and hits 103. Damn! He concludes now there is only one approach, and that is to wait it out. Not only is the short cycle top past due, but after this much of a rally, there is bound to be profit taking which will at least pull the price back some and allow getting out at a better price. He waits for the next day's opening.

The next day the copper market shows continuing strength. Is this possible? Better close at least half the position and then wait it out. He closes half the position at 103.50 (day 166). During the day, it sells off to 102.90 and then closes at 103.65. Finally some sign of selling pressure.

He sweats through the next day while the price makes a higher high and a lower low and then closes just 0.05 below the previous days close. He remembers reading somebody's method where this is taken as a key reversal, and he can now be sure that the next day will see some selling off. Anyway, now the 4-day indicator is showing signs of turning, so the strategy now is to wait for the short-term cycle bottom and then reverse the trade wherever the price is at that time.

On day 168, the price is rallying again; this now hopeless situation can only be resolved by taking the painful loss, and Ralph closes his position 104.10. He could then only look back over the previous six or seven days and feel rotten about the way he had been sucked in. And while he was reflecting on this, the price and the indicators turned up sharply on day 172 and the possible opportunity to profit on the long side had slipped by.

The loss trap had gotten him good! Had he simply followed the rules, the short trade would have been closed on day 162, or at the latest, on day 166. In either case, the trade would have been at a profit or about break-even. Not only had he allowed this to become a loss, he had added to the position thereby increasing the loss, and he had also missed a good opportunity on a long position.

The lessons from this not-so-unusual story are mostly obvious. The key, of course, is to follow the rules. Don't hold a position against the indicators. Don't ignore a stop-loss point, and when the price is threatening to reach a stop-loss point, put the order into the market. A mental stop point is easily passed by. Don't expect the market to behave according to **your** expectations. And, don't mix in rules from other systems as rationalizations for your mistakes. Sometimes cycle lengths fall at the extremes of the range. Still, the indicators and the stop-loss point can keep you out of trouble. And it is also very important to see how the situation developed so that Ralph didn't have full realization of the trap he was in until he was full-on into it. Don't let this happen to you.

6

Windmills of the
Mind
or
Trader Psychology

■ ■ ■

If one advances confidently in the direction of his dreams, and endeavors to live the life which he has imagined, he will meet with a success unexpected in the common hours.

Henry David Thoreau

The importance of the psychological aspects of trading were pointed out in Chapter 1, and some of the important characteristics of the successful trader were discussed. It was discussed early in the book to place in your mind the proper backdrop for the presentation of the development and application of the methodology. To quote a commodity trading advisor, Raymond Kaider (1988), "Often a trade is as much a battle against human nature as it will be against the market."

But taken in the abstract, the psychology of trading can seem sterile and not terribly relevant to the "important" aspect of learning how to make money. Now with the methodology in place and some trading (real or simulated) behind you, it can have more relevance.

6.1 KNOWING AND BELIEVING

You can read a dozen books on a subject and still not know it in the way you can know something that you have experienced first hand. For the most part, reading something involves only a small part of your being, mostly what Pearce[1] called the "roof brain." It is where you just think about things. It is just the current-conscious-thought part of the mind where many thoughts get bounced around every minute. You may believe something that you read, but you don't know it.

The next level involves the use of imagination, or what might be called "visualization." You can get some of this in your reading (studying) when you put yourself, by visualization, into the actual situation. You then can begin to activate a degree of the emotional, or the "feeling," part of the experience and some larger part of your person becomes involved. From this kind of experiencing, you can learn how you might react in a real situation.

Actual experience of situations, particularly those which have the potential for some real impact upon your life; in other words, those that can generate stress, involve all kinds of levels beyond that which you can experience vicariously. Complicated sets of psychological and emotional factors become involved. These are things that we may call subconscious, or at least unconscious; i.e., all those things that we are not conscious of at any given moment. They affect your whole person, mind and body, and determine the ways in which you respond. And some of the ways in which you might respond may surprise you.

---

[1]   Joseph Chilton Pearce, *Exploring the Crack in the Cosmic Egg,* New York, NY: Washington Square Press/Pocket Books, 1971.

This is certainly true in speculative trading. For most people, certainly in the beginning, speculative trading is a stressful, exciting activity which involves the whole personality. For this reason, it is important to realize the significance of the psychological factors, and to try to sense how you would react to trading situations before you actually experience them.

It is also important to realize that you probably can't really know until you actually have some experience. This will cause you to first study what you can, then to proceed with caution, and finally come back and study again after you have some experience and a changed perspective on what you are reading.

Some of the fundamentals of what we are calling psychological factors were presented in Chapter 1, and it is worth reviewing those to stress their importance. But the real significance can only be appreciated after gaining some better understanding of what is involved in trading, and then not until some actual experience has been accrued. That is why we want to come back to it here near the end; and because, if you are still pursuing the study at this point, you are probably serious about trading.

6.2 COMMITMENT

We've heard a lot about commitment, but it is usually in the context of a relationship, not investing. But in the context of trading, it is important for two reasons: you must make a commitment to trading, never to a particular trade.

Before you commit any money to trading, you need to examine the extent to which you are committed to trading. Most people approach trading as a sort of hobby—something that they can do on the side. They want to continue being doctors, lawyers, engineers or whatever and make money trading as a hobby.There is little chance that it is going to be successful. They might believe that they would "like" to make their living as a trader, but want to know first whether or not it is going to work. Would you go to a doctor that practiced medicine as a hobby?

This is not to suggest that you can't continue your current occupation and still trade successfully. However, during the learning phase, or if you intend to develop some of your own methods, your current occupation cannot be highly demanding upon your time, and you must be sufficiently able and motivated to consider that you can handle two professions.

After you become proficient at trading, at least for the type of trading that is suggested with the system in this book, you will find that it is a part-time activity and that you can do other things. After all, trading is mostly waiting. But you must be able to give it your attention when it is demanded.

The ultimate measure of your level of commitment is the relative success of your trading over the long term. Even experienced and successful traders are subject to periods when external distractions and internal conflicts reduce their effectiveness in dealing with trading decisions. It is their continuing commitment that forces a self-examination to understand the potential obstacles to consistent success.

The major commitment of time is in the early stages of becoming a trader. This can be from many months to many years. You must study the markets and the methods, and you must engage in self-analysis to understand how to deal with the market and the methods in a calm, confident and objective fashion. But both the method and the emotions require on-going commitment to review and analysis of the problems. You will run into different problems at different stages in your trading. I have lost count of the number of times I was sure that I had things wired only to find another obstacle later on. And, of course, some lessons seem to need learning over and over.

Most of the problems that arise will be the problems in the trader's head. It may seem simplistic, but the two objectives of trading, i.e., making profits and avoiding losses, are in themselves the biggest triggers of psychological obstacles. The strong desire to avoid losses becomes the reason that losses are not taken when they are small, and they become large. Having a nice profit triggers premature closure of the trade as the excitement of the gain, and the fear of again losing it, overwhelm objectivity, and you take much less profit than the trade could have produced.

So, in its simplest form, commitment in trading is committing to follow all the rules of the method; totally objective, no preconceived notions, no fear and no greed. It is that easy, and it is that difficult.

Like the man from La Mancha, we will find ourselves sparing with windmills that seem to appear from nowhere, have no basis in our logic, but obstruct our path to consistent profits. However, it is not a Quixotic venture. If you have really committed yourself to becoming a trader you will persevere, and the windmills will become fewer, smaller and more distant.

What about never committing to a particular trade? The making of a trade is based upon the information you have **now**. Your expectation may be, because of the average length of the cycle you're trading, that this trade will be on for about 7 days or 10 days. But don't ever commit to holding a trade for a particular period of time, or to a given amount of profit. The information may indicate the trade be closed tomorrow, or 10 minutes from now.

Committing to a trade, which usually means staying with it even when you have evidence that it is going wrong, can result from the "certainty trap." The essence of the certainty trap is disregarding the level of risk involved by over-estimating the degree of certainty of the information upon which you base your decisions. Taking risks is an inherent part of life; it's only dangerous when you act like you're not taking a risk.

The degree of certainty with which you enter a trade does vary, but don't ever believe it's a sure thing.

6.3 "PRACTICE" TRADING

When I first developed the reactivity indicator, I gathered years of historical data on the stock market indices, calculated the indicators and printed out plots of index price and the indicators. I carefully taped all of these together so that I could lay them out across the room and compare the turning points in the indicators and the price data. Marking all the buy and sell points, I could then go back and compute how much money I would have made by buying call and put options on the index. No doubt about it, the profits were going to be huge.

After some months of actual trading, I found that I wasn't making any money. What could possibly be wrong?

Somewhere in the back of my mind, I knew that I had perhaps cheated just a little at some of the decision points. I was looking at the charts both past and future. I had preconceived notions, and they were always right. At the places where it wasn't clear from the indicators what to do, I always made the right choice and perhaps even made the choices a little more timely then ever possible in real life.

This kind of paper trading is not at all representative of actual trading and is worse than useless as practice, it is negative. It sets up expectations that are entirely unrealistic which can make things difficult later when nothing even approaching the expectation is realized. As a purely objective examination of indicator behavior, it can be informative, but it is not practice trading.

Later, after having given up trading options, and having gained futures trading experience in actual trading, I devised another way to practice trade. With slight modification of the actual trading spreadsheet, I could incorporate historical data that was kept off the screen, and copy it into the spreadsheet one day at a time. After each day's data was entered and calculated, I could examine the graphs and make any trade decisions necessary. This seemed to me to be representative of the real situation.

Still, my practice results were clearly better than my actual trading performance. This clearly pointed out the importance of those "unconscious" factors.

Although this practice, or testing, was methodologically sound, all of the psychological factors were missing. There was no money involved; therefore there was no fear, no greed, and no pressure. There was no "real time" involved; therefore there was no time to worry and no time to second guess. So there was absolutely no stress; except, of course, for the excitement of how wonderfully the system worked.

But practice trading is important. The musician, the athlete, the artist, even the farmer become good at what they do by practice, practice, practice. And the quarterback doesn't just hone his skills during Sunday's game. However, practice can only be helpful if it is the right kind of practice.

Setting up the "blind data" approach is a good way to test your trading of a commodity you haven't traded before, and it is good practice. The fact that the psychological factors **are** missing makes it of real value. It gives the experience of making trades in an objective fashion. You get to know what it "feels" like to trade without the hampering effects of the psychological factors. You can then carry this into your actual trading.

When you find yourself in a real quandary about an important trade and realize that the stress factors are operative, you can ask "What would I do if I were practice trading?" It helps.

The difference in the degree of success that you achieve in practice vs your actual trading might give you a clue to the extent that your psychology is interfering with your methodology. If you don't achieve profits when practice trading, don't trade.

The way to do practice trading is to set up an approach which simulates as closely as possible the methodological aspects of trading. Use historical data and enter it into your analysis one day at a time in a way which does not allow seeing the data in advance. Examine the indicators, and make your trade decisions just as you would in real trading and keep a tabulation of your trades. And when you go back to evaluate profits and losses, be sure to include commissions and fees.

6.4 STRESS BUILDERS

There is a lot of discussion of stress these days. Is there actually more stress, or is it that we are simply more aware of it and what to call it? Perhaps it is just that it is necessarily dealt with a different way; a way that doesn't relieve it.

The condition we have come to know as stress derives from a primal response to a real or perceived threat. It was very helpful to our survival, as it is for animals in the wild. The stress resulted in actual physiological changes, having a lot to do with the production of adrenaline, which allowed us to run away faster, or to fight with greater strength.

There are many situations in which we may still find ourselves where the stress, and its effect on our performance, is beneficial. But because of the different condition of our lives, the degree of control exercised upon our environment and the type of challenges which we face, in many cases, stress degrades our performance, and if chronic, can be physically harmful.

The biological reaction to stress results in a focusing of our energies and abilities into a few options, and allows us to do them with greater force. Using the primitive example, we could run faster without noticing pain in our feet, climb a tree faster, jump a wider stream, whatever, until we were safe. The biological effects would be worn off through physical exercise, and when we were safe we could relax completely.

Now as we are stressed by events or other people, we sit at our desks or at our computer screens and try to work harder. Unfortunately, the effects of the stress usually make us less effective because it narrows our perspective, thereby reducing the options that we consider.

Try to perform well in a pressure situation while sitting at your desk with your supervisor looking over your shoulder. The stress does not get applied to any physical response; you will not run away, nor will you attack your boss. We can only deal with it "intellectually," and in the absence of working it off physically, it has a way of being internalized.

In addition to causing us to focus on fewer options, stress also has an apparent effect of expanding the time scale; that is, it seems like a lot more time is passing than really is. You've heard people relating that during periods of extreme stress "minutes seemed like hours."

There becomes a sense of urgency that some action must be taken **now**, even when a half hour from now may be fine, or perhaps no action should be taken at all. It is the need to relieve the stress by taking some kind of action that the action becomes so important. The trader making a trade based upon this stress-induced combination of a narrowed perspective and the need to relieve some stress by taking immediate action is not likely to be making consistently good trades.

You need only to consider these factors for awhile to see how your behavior in trading situations can be affected by stress. When a potentially large sum of money is at stake, be it a potential profit or a loss, it can become difficult to make objective consideration of all factors and take calm action.

So it is evident that for most of us, some consideration must be made of this stress issue to better understand what makes it happen and how to deal with it. I will consider the stress builders from the point of view of the trader to be uncertainty, worry, and fear and their inter-relationships. Although the progression is probably uncertainty, worry, fear, and leading to stress, I think they may be best understood in reverse order.

Fear

It seems to me that the distilled basis for stress is fear. In trading, it is the fear of losing, the fear of being wrong, the fear of missing an opportunity, or the fear of allowing a profit to get away. It may be called something else; like misjudging probabilities, or inability to make a decision, or maybe just "hoping." But mostly it has to do with being afraid at some level. And, of course, fear is the springboard for that "fight or flight" syndrome mentioned above, and gets the adrenaline flowing.

Be aware of your mental and emotional condition when you are trading. When stress levels rise, try to determine what it is that you are "afraid" might result from what **is** happening, or from what **might** happen. Consider what the options are that you can consider. Above all, stay within the criteria of the trading system. Relying upon the system and taking the action demanded by its rules, no matter how difficult, is the best way to reduce stress in a trading situation.

There is an equivalence between desire and fear. The more strongly you want something, the more you are afraid that you will not get it, or if you have it, that you might lose it. Reduce the desire and reduce the fear. Don't get your heart set on making a lot of money in your trading or in a particular trade. Just take the approach of making **some** money; take what the market and the method will give you.

Taking what the markets give you within the system you are trading also means taking the losses that are within the system. And don't try to scale up the number of contracts you are trading too quickly after making some profits. Take a patient and gradual approach.

Worry

Worry and fear are obviously closely related and perhaps the way in which you see them is a matter of semantics. I see worry as a precursor to fear, or a fear on a more conceptual basis. Worry is the conceptualizing of many possible negative outcomes or events which **haven't yet happened**, and most likely **never will happen**. They are usually exaggerated negative outcomes. And these possible negative outcomes become "realized" in our minds and trigger the fear response and resultant stress.

Worry may be culturally induced in that we are taught to anticipate all the possible things that can go wrong so that we can be prepared to deal with them. But notice the negative bias. There are obviously just as many possible things that are going to be right. Don't we also have to be prepared to deal with things that go right? We simply assume that if events happen as we like, we will know exactly what to do next. We are **confident**.

There is a difference between worrying and planning. Planning is more of an objective ordering of future events in order to set a direction or intent. Unexpected events of both a positive and negative nature will occur, and they are dealt with as we proceed. In the context of trading, worry is primarily a fear of poor performance. One way that you can reduce worry is to develop confidence that you will know how to handle events as they occur. When you find yourself growing the "worry tree," that is, trying to analyze all the various branches of possible negative future outcomes, cut it off now. Deal with the factual information of current reality.

Worrying has a double negative effect. While a portion of the mental processing capacity is occupied with worry, it is not available to broaden our awareness of what is happening now. And as we trigger the fear response to the imagined negative outcomes, we suffer the stress effects discussed above in relation to fear. Because the number of possible future outcomes builds geometrically, we don't have to project far into the future before our processing capacity is almost totally occupied with outcomes that will never happen.

So the two effects are working to strangle our ability to objectively consider current options. While the growing worry tree is occupying more of our processing ability, the overall capacity for processing is being narrowed because of the focusing effects of stress. In the extreme, we are immobilized.

Don't allow yourself to be seriously hampered by worry-induced stress. As soon as you become aware that your mind is spinning on things that haven't yet happened, and it is impairing your ability for objective consideration, say aloud "stop!" Go look out the window. Take some slow controlled deep breaths. Focus on a sense of well-being. Then determine if some action is appropriate and do it. If not, forget about it for now.

People have often asked me, "Aren't you worried about holding positions overnight or over the weekend?" Not at all. I don't think about them because, after all, the market is closed and there is absolutely nothing I can do about it until the market opens. And when the market opens, I will have some new information, and I will then consider whether or not there is anything that should be done. And of course any event that may occur while the market is closed that will affect the price is just as likely to affect it in my favor as to the contrary.

Uncertainty

Just as worry may be a precursor to fear, uncertainty is a precursor to worry. Worry has two essential ingredients, uncertainty and time. When it is clear what is going to happen next or what action you should take, there is little to worry about. Or even if there is considerable uncertainty, if it only lasts a short time, we usually let things take their course before we generate a base of worry.

But when things are uncertain for longer periods of time, the mind generates "the worry tree," and we find ourselves preoccupied with following all of the various branches of possible outcomes, usually negative, until the discomfort level becomes considerable.

It is this discomfort level that seems to "force" traders to make unnecessary and unprofitable decisions. This is one reason why the method you're using works better in practice trading than in actual trading. Even when there is uncertainty about what to do, you are able to go on to the next day's data without taking an incorrect action because you haven't had time to worry.

Many people find uncertainty to be frightening and stressful. On a larger scale than the individual trade, traders who have given up a corporate career to trade find the lack of a corporate structure in their lives to be uncomfortable. Particularly with some degree of success in trading, the subsequent freedom, which is exactly what they were after, becomes stressful because of the number of options open to them at any moment.

Excitement

Excitement is a type of stress builder that also leads to stimulated action and the flow of adrenaline. It is probably the opposite of worry in the sense that it is the result of positive outcomes, and the expectation of continued positive outcomes, combined with the fear of losing the positive outcome. But just like worry, it can lead to distorted perceptions and actions that are detrimental to overall trading results. This may be the operative stress builder for the compulsive gambler.

It can be the most insidious because it is more like an addiction. As worry may be an exaggerated negative feeling, excitement is an exaggerated positive feeling. And we know that positive reinforcement is the more powerful of the two. From my own personal experience, I know that the excitement over winning trades made the memory of them so overshadow the losses that I would forget the losing trades. Over a period of days or weeks, I would have the strong impression that I was winning, but when I would bring my accounting up to date I would find that it wasn't true.

It's excitement that makes "random reinforcement" such a powerful conditioning mechanism, and it is certainly operative in trading. An animal doesn't need to be given a reward every time it does the desired behavior. It will continue doing the behavior as long as it is occasionally rewarded.

All that is needed to make us continue a trading practice that is not consistent with our system is to have it work well sometimes. Even though the net result over many of these trades is negative, it is difficult not to try again because sometimes it works. This is why traders keep trying to pick tops and bottoms ahead of the signals given by the method being used.

6.5 CHOICES AND RESPONSIBILITY

It was previously mentioned that a key characteristic of the successful trader is responsibility. However the trade goes, you made the choices that led to that trade. If things go wrong, like taking a loss, there is a tendency to find some other reasons for the loss; the guys on the floor went after your stop-loss order, your broker influenced you, or the arbitrage traders are messing it up for the rest of us.

As long as you allow yourself to feel that someone/something else is to blame for the negative outcome, you are not attributing it to choices that you made. This is being the "victim." The victim has no responsibility for what happened and will continue to go on making the same mistakes again.

If you choose to trade, this is your game and you accept all the vagaries with it. So when things go wrong, don't blame anybody. That means you don't blame yourself either. You go back to the point where you made the decision to enter the trade. Review the information that you had, the data and the indicators, and even try to reconstruct the emotional content of what was going on at the time.

Then look at other alternatives that you might have considered at the time. If you had other choices consistent with the rules of the method, evaluate what the potential outcomes would have been. If there is one that you like better than the one you actually chose, remember it for next time. Practice this with each trade and you will learn to make better choices. Each trade that you do not handle properly is simply a learning experience that allows you to do better the next time.

6.6 DEALING WITH PROFITS AND LOSSES

The most difficult aspect of trading is dealing with losses. It is very uncomfortable psychologically, and many hidden factors come into play which make it difficult to take the loss when it should be taken, when it is still small. But dealing with profits is also difficult. There are many factors here which tend to cause traders to take profits early, and thereby take less than full advantage of a trade, or to hold on too long while waiting for a larger profit.

In its simplest form, the faulted trader mentality regarding taking profits is illustrated by a story attributed to Fred Kelly, author of *Why You Win or Lose*. It seems a young boy was walking along a trail when he spotted an old man trying to trap wild turkeys. The man had a trap which was a simple contrivance consisting of a big box with a door hinged at the top. The door was kept open by a prop to which some twine was tied leading back to the operator a hundred feet or so away.

A trail of corn was scattered along a path to lure the turkeys into the box. Once inside the turkeys found a plentiful supply of corn. When enough turkeys had made their way into the box, the man would simply jerk away the prop letting the door fall shut trapping the turkeys in the box. Of course, any still outside the box would be frightened away. The time to pull away the prop was when as many turkeys were inside the box as one could reasonably expect.

At one point the man had a dozen turkeys in the box. Then one wandered back out. "Gosh, I wish I had pulled the string when all 12 were there," said the old man. "I'll wait a minute and maybe that one will go back in."

But while he waited for the twelfth turkey to return, two more walked out. "I should have been satisfied with 11," the trapper said. "Just as soon as I get one more back, I'll pull the string."

But then, three more came back out. Still the man waited, hoping some of them would go back in. Having had 12 turkeys at one point, he really disliked the idea of going home with less than eight. **He couldn't give up the idea that some of the original number would return.**

While he kept on hoping that more would return, they had all come out but one. In desperation he finally said, "I'll wait until he walks out or another one goes in, and then I'll quit." The solitary turkey went out to join the others, and the man went home empty-handed.

This story aptly illustrates the psychological factors that come into play with both profits and losses, and illustrates the need for following a disciplined system for knowing when to close a trade. Stop counting turkeys, and pay attention to the indicators.

The Loss Trap

Dealing with losses can involve the same psychology as the turkey trap. A position has gone against you, but you hesitate in getting out while you hope that it will turn back in your favor. As the loss gets worse, you become more and more afraid to take the loss because of what it will do to your overall balance sheet. Finally, you are sure that it is unlikely that it can go any further against you without some bounce-back, at which time you intend to get out. But as it does bounce back you hesitate some more while you hope that it is now going your way.

When the pain of the loss finally becomes so excruciating that you can deny it no longer, you close the trade. And as though it were some kind of a dastardly plot of the markets, it is likely that this is near the point where the price turns. It is not so surprising. There are a lot of other speculators behaving in this same way. It is this changing of positions that is helping the price to turn. The errant traders are getting out while the smart ones are getting in. This whole process was illustrated by the example in section 5.6.

So, it is critical that you get a hold of yourself right away. By far the most stressful thing about trading commodities is sitting with a losing position for which the rules of the method would have you out, either by evidence of the indicators or the stop-loss point. Take the loss just as soon as you have solid reason to do so, and be ready to re-enter with the smart money.

The more the trader resists taking the sure loss, the more he becomes ensnared in the psychological traps that keep him locked into it. The longer he struggles with the loss, the worse the loss becomes. The only way to get out of the trap is to let go of the trade. Don't let it financially cripple you.

In addition to the financial effect of letting a loss grow large is the crippling effect that it can have on your self-confidence. Taking a large loss and finally exiting a trade near the turn in the market can be devastating. You lose your confidence and courage that are so critical to taking the decisive actions necessary to get into the next trade.

Follow the method getting in, and follow the method getting out. Don't deceive yourself that this time you know better than the method. It is not a question of admitting being wrong. Let the method take the responsibility for the trade. That is how to avoid the loss trap.

Profit Anxiety

For the most part, profits are pretty comfortable. This is the fun part about trading—letting the profits run. But the markets are not so well behaved that there aren't set-backs in these positions that cause anxiety. It is particularly troublesome as pull-backs occur near an anticipated trade point. The trader can get anxious to try to pick the exact end-point of the price move, expecting to maximize the profit.

The two principal scenarios are these. As uncertainty sets in near the turning point, and the trade is at a handsome profit, the tendency is strong to take it. After all, you are happy with it, and nobody can argue with a nice profit. Taking a profit before the indication by the rules of the method may occasionally give you a slightly larger profit than waiting for the signal. That's what reinforces this behavior. But there are many more times when the move resumes strongly in the direction of your trade, and you have only realized a portion of the potential.

The other common tendency is to wait too long—to hesitate after the signal because you have some notion that the move hasn't ended. This is particularly true when the move has been small, and you can't accept that it's over and that's all there is. Again, on the average, the best course of action is to stick with the rules.

It is important to recognize that it is not sufficient to just make a profit on a trade. For your profits to significantly outweigh the losses, you must get all the potential there is to a given trade. Your trades may be wrong more than they are right and still make handsome profits if the average profit far exceeds the average loss.

I once knew an option trader who closed his trades when his profit reached $1,000 or returned to zero, whichever came first. He never let his losses exceed $1,000. The assumption was that if he was right more than half the time, he would win. The combination of commissions and less than 50 percent of good trades kept his trading career rather short.

6.7 CONSCIOUS VERSUS SUBCONSCIOUS—WHO IS IN CONTROL HERE?

An important concept to understand in dealing with our behavior is the division of conscious and subconscious activity, and how our behavior is affected by each.[2] As defined earlier, we will consider "conscious" to include all of those things that you are aware of at any time, as now you are aware of the words you are reading on this page, and maybe some other distraction. There is definitely a limited amount of information that we can consciously deal with at any one time. The "subconscious" (or "unconscious" if you prefer) is everything else about ourselves and our environment.

The conscious mind is a small part of "mind." It may be where we think, the intellectual and rational activity, and it may appear that it is in control of our behavior, but actually it only plays a part. The subconscious mind is not so limited in its capacity, and it controls our behavior in ways in which we may be totally unaware.

Even though you may have the best of trading systems, one that works like a money machine when you practice trade, you may find yourself looking back upon a losing trade and asking yourself, "Why on earth did I do that?" Or on a broader scale than individual trades, you may find one or more of the following symptoms:

---

2   Tharp, Van K., Ph.D., "Dealing with Conflict," *Stocks and Commodities*, November, 1988.

- You have a period of successful trading and you have made a certain amount of money, say $50,000 or $100,000, and you suddenly find that you are no longer following the system exactly, and you are taking a string of losses. A certain ceiling has been reached and for unknown reasons, you can no longer trade effectively.

- You feel negative about yourself and negative about your trading activity, perhaps feeling that it is not a worthwhile occupation and the source of these feelings is not apparent.

- You know the system works if you just follow it, but for some reason you always want to do better and make trades prior to the signal.

- Your system signals a trade but you expect a move in the opposite direction and you miss a big move, or you make a bad trade in addition to missing the move by being on the wrong side.

- You make money easily when trading your own account, but have difficulty in trading accounts for others, or vice-versa.

- You worry excessively about your positions to the point where you can't think about anything else and can't sleep, even though you have handled greater risk positions comfortably in the past.

These are just a few samples of the kinds of symptoms that traders experience that are a result of subconscious factors. It is important to examine your trading activity to see if you can identify certain behavior patterns, certain problems that are limiting your trading success, and resolve the subconscious forces that are causing these behaviors.

You know that there are many activities that you do that you don't have to "think" about. When you first learned to drive you were conscious of every action you made: shifting into gear, pressing the accelerator, steering, etc., and you weren't good at it. Now you may drive for miles while thinking of something else entirely and not have any conscious awareness of getting there.

The subconscious has much greater capacity of information and background, and deals with a myriad of factors not available to the conscious; therefore, it generally controls your behavior. Not all of these factors are favorable for trading.

Going back to our discussion of the stress factors above, we saw that the capacity for considering alternatives (a conscious activity) was narrowed by stress. The narrowing of the conscious activities puts the subconscious more in control. Many of the subconscious factors that can influence our trading behavior have nothing whatsoever to do directly with the trade.

Many of these subconscious factors are mechanisms that we have built-in during our lives to provide a seemingly positive function, e.g.:

- To help you get attention, or approval, from others
- To protect you from painful memories
- To keep your pride from being hurt or protect you from failure
- To help you survive in an emergency
- To provide self-motivation
- To steer you toward self-satisfaction

These mechanisms, operating outside of your awareness, may produce behavior that is contrary to good trading behavior, and contrary to what your conscious mind sees as desirable. There are then two actions that need be taken to improve our trading results; teach (or perhaps "re-program") the subconscious, and resolve conflicts between different aspects of the subconscious, and between the conscious and subconscious.

Teaching the Subconscious

Re-programming the subconscious introduces the need for a bridge, or link, between conscious and subconscious. This is sometimes called the "preconscious," or as Louis Tice, in his seminar and audio tape series "New Age Thinking," talks about it as the "creative subconscious." This is the part that he says "automatically produces the behavior that is consistent with your self-image." This is the foundation for the approach of visualizing the desired behavior or outcome in a repeated and vivid way, and having the subconscious produce that behavior, or make the desired outcome a reality. A psychologist may refer to this as "guided imagery."

In trading, the approach is not to visualize yourself with lots of money and living the good life, although that might be a secondary result. Stick to the primary action that is most directly influenced by subconscious behavior. Visualize the behavior that you can control. To improve your trading results, visualize yourself confidently and consistently acting in accordance with the trading method.

This is where the practice trading discussed above can be valuable. It can provide you with an image of yourself trading in keeping with all the rules of the method and the money management, and doing it without stress and second guessing. Since this is not real time trading, you must mentally add the patience required to wait for the market to tell you what to do.

Every day, take a quiet moment to vividly visualize yourself confidently making the trade required by your system, whatever it is, while keeping in full view the alternatives available in making your decisions. Let the money and profits take care of themselves, you are just making the trades as required by your system.

Resolving the Conflicts

The conflict of conscious factors and subconscious factors can make trading stressful and lead to trading mistakes. It is important, and sometimes difficult, to be specific about what these conflicts are in order to work at their resolution.

Generally the conscious part of the dilemma has to do with the interpretation of the trading data. When some subconscious conflict is present, you will find yourself finding strong reasons to make conclusions that go beyond what your trading system is telling you. You may have a strong sense that you know something that the indicators are not yet telling you; perhaps, that if you don't act now, you will be missing an opportunity. Or, the indicators may call for a trade, and you are not able to take action, particularly when it is time to cut a loss.

One method for dealing with the subconscious conflicts makes use of the "parts model," and then carrying on a sort of "negotiation" between the parts in order to neutralize the conflict (Van K. Tharp, 1988, previously referenced). One part of you might work to protect you from failure, so it causes you to procrastinate because of the risk involved in a money-making trade opportunity. Another part of you may protect your self-esteem and not allow you to accept losses quickly, thus forcing you to take a large loss later. Still another part wants you to be "right" and generates expectations about the market which often conflict with the signals generated by your system. So, you see how there can be conflict between the behavior generated by these various parts.

Serious losses can occur when a part of you satisfies some positive intention that is not appropriate in the context of winning in the market. And at times, ignoring or overriding the signals from some part can result in more dramatic behavior which forces your attention to certain other aspects.

The key is to pay attention to the feelings of conflict and try to identify the possible causes. In my personal experience, it took me some time to identify a conflict between the strongly intuitive part of me and the analytical/objective part. The intuitive part has served me well in adding insight and a sense of direction in which to proceed when engaged in creative problem solving, such as in development of the methods described in this book. But following the method clearly requires objectivity.

The negotiation resulted in an understanding that intuition into how things have worked, or are working now, is different than projecting into an unknown future in the commodity markets. In fact, the behavior of the markets seems many times to be entirely contrary to intuitive expectations. The intuitive part had to accept that it played its role in the development of the methods, and it is up to the objective part to carry out those methods.

It may seem strange to speak of these different aspects of mind as though they each were a separate whole entity, but it is at least a tool for resolution of problems and further developing understanding of behavior. A more elaborate procedure for negotiating between parts is given by Dr. Van K. Tharp in his article.

As a last thought on all this methodology and psychology, one might consider the "incompleteness theorems" developed by a famous Austrian mathematician, Kurt Gödel. In simplified form they tell us two things: (1) a logical system that has any degree of sophistication can never be complete, and (2) nor can it even be guaranteed to be consistent.

At the risk of becoming too philosophical, in this last chapter our preoccupation has been with the mind thinking about itself. The problem is that it only has *itself* to think about itself *with*. To think about the mind, one has to employ the mind. In this situation, the mind must serve as both the "observed" and the "observer." By stepping outside the mind in order to observe it, something necessarily must have been withdrawn, and this will affect any future observation of it. By the inherent process of thinking about the mind *with* the mind, both the completeness and the consistency of our reasoning are likely to suffer.

In any case, we now have assembled some of the three ingredients: the methodology, the money management, and the trader psychology. With persistence, patience, a measure of self-forgiveness when we make a mistake, and more persistence, we can achieve the goal of high-return futures trading.

Good Trading!

Appendix A

The Workings of the Commodity Markets

∎ ∎ ∎

The primary function of the commodity exchanges is to provide a market-place wherein producers, processors, manufacturers, distributors, import-ers, exporters and other handlers of commodities may hedge the risk of inventory loss because of price changes during the period of ownership of the physical commodity. Hedge means to "offset." To best illustrate a series of hedges, we will go through an involved example which tracks the use of futures contracts to hedge a wheat crop from the farmer to the end user.

THE FARMER

During the month of January, a wheat farmer sits down and calculates the cost of producing his winter wheat crop. He includes his expense for seed, fertilizer, fuel, labor, land cost, machinery depreciation, interest on loans, etc., and the shipping cost to deliver his wheat to Chicago. After estimating his yield, he finds that the total cost is $3.60 per bushel.

He notes that, at that time, the wheat futures contract for July delivery are trading at $3.80. He instructs his commodity broker to execute (sell) futures contracts totaling something close to the amount that he expects to produce. By doing so, he has guaranteed himself a profit of $.20 per bushel, and he has very little further concern for the fluctuation in the price of wheat. His crop is hedged, and he has assured himself a profit.

By the time he has harvested his crop in late May, he may decide that the cash price at the local grain elevator is attractive and he doesn't want to store the grain and subsequently ship it to Chicago. So he hauls it directly from the field and sells it to the local elevator. He no longer needs the hedge and does not have the wheat for July delivery, so he will lift the hedge by instructing his broker to cover the position by making offsetting contracts (buy) in an amount equal to the original hedge.

The initial contract was to deliver (sell) a certain number of bushels of wheat in July at Chicago; the offsetting position was to take delivery (buy) the same number of bushels of wheat in July in Chicago. One cancels the other, and the farmer has no further obligation.

During the time that the farmer was hedged, he had eliminated the risk of price fluctuations. For while a rise in the price of wheat would cause him to lose money on his futures contract, the loss would be offset by the increase in the value of his physical wheat. The opposite is also true; a decline in the price of wheat would result in a profit on his futures contracts and a corresponding loss on the physical wheat. The farmer was satisfied with a profit of $.20 a bushel, and he had guaranteed that profit in January, probably before the crop started to grow.

THE GRAIN ELEVATOR OPERATOR

When the farmer sells his wheat to the local grain elevator operator, the elevator operator has assumed the risk of ownership. Since the elevator operator is in the business of storing grains for the storage charges only, and has no interest (generally) in speculating on the price fluctuations, he will now hedge his position.

In total, the elevator operator may have purchased as much as a million bushels of wheat. If he does not hedge that position and the price of wheat declines only $.10 per bushel (a fairly modest price change for wheat), the elevator operator could lose $100,000 on his million bushels of wheat—a catastrophic loss. Therefore, like the farmer, the elevator operator will hedge his inventory risk by selling futures contracts for an amount equal to his inventory.

Once he is hedged, he has little concern for the fluctuation in the price of wheat, since gains and losses in the cash price for physical wheat will be offset by corresponding losses or gains in his futures contracts. As time passes and the elevator operator sells wheat from his inventory, he will lift portions of his hedge so that he stays equally hedged between physical inventory and futures contracts.

THE MILLER

Among the customers who may be buying wheat from the grain elevator operator might be a miller who will grind the wheat into baking flour. The miller may be making contractual arrangements with his customers to deliver flour many months from now at specific prices. If the miller does not hedge against these contracts he may suffer substantial losses if the price of wheat advances sharply before he is able to buy the wheat necessary for grinding to meet his contractual obligations.

Like the farmer and the grain elevator operator, the miller will also hedge to avoid risk, but his hedge will be opposite to theirs. The first two hedges were selling hedges since the farmer and the elevator operator had the commodity in their possession. The miller's hedge will be a buying hedge because he will be buying to guarantee acquisition of the physical commodity at a future date, at a specific price, which will enable him to meet his contractual obligations profitably.

Once the miller has hedged his position, he also has no further concern for the price fluctuations in wheat. Again, inventory losses or gains will be offset by corresponding gains or losses on his futures contracts.

THE BAKER

Meanwhile, the baker, who will buy the flour from the miller, is making commitments for delivery of bread, cakes and other goods at some future date, so he must also hedge against these commitments by making buying hedges. His inventory gains or losses will also be offset by corresponding gains or losses on his futures contracts.

If it were not for the benefit of the price protection offered by hedging, users of wheat would be forced to trade with higher markups to offset the increased risks of unforeseen price fluctuations. The price swings of wheat because of poor growing conditions, or excess production, can be sizeable. In 1988, the price of Chicago wheat increased more than $1.00 per bushel in about six months.

THE SPECULATOR

To further reduce the day-to-day or minute-to-minute price swings by adding liquidity to the markets, another type of commodity trader has been invited to trade. He/she is known as the speculator. He rarely owns or ever deals in the physical commodity, but he speculates on what he believes the price changes will be. Besides adding liquidity to the markets, he, in effect, takes a portion of the risk that has been laid off by the producer and users discussed above.

If the speculator believes the price of wheat may rise, he makes a contract to *take* delivery of (to buy) wheat in Chicago at a specific price on a specific date. He has no intention of ever taking delivery of the wheat, so sometime before the delivery date arrives, he will make an offsetting contract to *make delivery* of (to sell) wheat in Chicago at a specific price on the originally specified date. One contract cancels the other, and the only matter to be settled is the profit or loss on his contracts. If the selling price is higher than the buying price, he has a profit, otherwise a loss.

The volume of trading accounted for by speculators is enormous and assists commodity users and producers in exchanging the physical commodity or manufactured product at the lowest possible prices.

THE PROCEDURE

The first requirement to trading commodities is to open an account with a broker who trades commodities. If the trader is going to make his own decisions about when and what to trade (highly advisable, and the purpose for this book), the obvious choice is a discount broker. It will require signing some forms, acknowledging that you are aware of the risks involved, and depositing some money, usually a minimum of $5,000.

Continuing with wheat, for illustration, suppose the trader has determined that the price of wheat may increase in the coming weeks or months. He will give the broker an order to buy one or more contracts of wheat. Each contract is 5,000 bushels. The logistics of the transaction are similar to a stock purchase. The broker sends the order to the floor of the exchange, and the trade is executed. The terms of the trade are communicated back to the broker for confirmation with the client.

There are two basic differences between the purchase of stock shares and purchase of a commodities' futures contract. The first is that the stock purchase is permanent so that the new owner may hold the stock for as long as he chooses; whereas, the commodity futures contract purchaser has merely made a *contract* to purchase and will not become an owner until the contract expires, if the contract has not been offset.

The second, and more important difference, lies in the use of the word "contract." The commodity futures contract buyer does not purchase anything physical. A wheat buyer does not actually buy any wheat. He makes a contract to buy wheat for delivery at a specified location on a specified date. So there is a very different meaning to the word "margin" in commodities than in stocks.

When buying a stock on margin, the buyer is borrowing money from the broker to make the purchase. The buyer must put up a certain percentage in cash, say 50 percent, as a down payment on the stock. In commodities, the margin required is more like "earnest" money, showing it is a good faith contract. It also provides some minimum room for the price of the commodity to move against the position after the purchase before more money must be available in the account, or the position closed.

If a speculator notes in September that the price of wheat for December delivery in Chicago is $3.80, and he has concluded that the price of wheat will be lower before December, he will instruct his broker to "sell five December Chicago wheat at $3.80 (or 'at market')." The speculator is making a contract to deliver 5,000 bushels of wheat in Chicago in December at $3.80 per bushel. Since he has no wheat to hedge, and no contracts to take delivery to offset, this is "short" selling.

Having executed this order, the client has until December to decide to make delivery of the wheat or to cancel the contract by entering into an offsetting buy contract. Obviously, the speculator doesn't intend to deliver any physical wheat, so when he concludes that the time/price is right—when December wheat is at $3.40 per bushel—he buys his contract. He instructs his broker to "buy five December Chicago wheat at $3.40 (or at 'market')." The buy and sell orders cancel each other out and the price difference represents the profit for the speculator.

In this case, assuming the orders were executed at the prices mentioned, he has a profit of $.40 per bushel, and on one contract of 5,000 bushels, the total profit is $2,000, less commissions and fees. The margin needed in the client's account to make this contract was probably less than $1,000, so the inherent return on money actually used was very high.

In the liquid markets provided by the exchanges, it is not necessary for parties on opposite sides of a trade to agree to offset their position simultaneously. There are many traders in the "pit" at the exchange at any one time, some representing the producers, shippers, millers, exporters, etc., and many pure speculators. Any trade may be executed at any time with any one of these who is willing to take the opposite side of the trade. As an off-the-floor trader ("outsider"), you will not trade with another outsider. Your trade will be made with someone on the floor—a "local."

The net number of contracts being held (not offset) at the close of the session is represented by the "open interest". As time goes by and the contract expiration day comes, the remaining contracts being held are by those who actually intend to make delivery, or to take delivery, of the physical commodity. Of course, before the expiration date for a given delivery comes, trading is going on in contracts for other delivery dates farther into the future.

Note from the discussion about buying and selling contracts that it is not necessary for the first transaction to be a "buy" order. It is just as easy, and requires the same margin, to make a "sell" order, as was the case with the hedgers. If the speculator anticipates a price decrease, he simply sells contracts and offsets them later by buying contracts. If the price has gone down, he has made a profit of the difference in the buy and sell price just as before. So the futures speculator doesn't care whether prices go up or down; he just wants them to move, and he wants to be on the right side.

PRICE CHANGES

It generally would take some significant period of time for the price of wheat to vary over a 40 cent range as given in the example. During that time, there will be many factors being considered by the participants in the market that will affect the price. These may include the following factors and their effects:

- A government report is issued, which indicates the recently harvested crop was larger than previously estimated. This increase in supply causes a drop in price.

- Word is circulated that the major southern hemisphere producers are having problems with their wheat crops. This indicates a possibility of a reduction in the overall world supply and causes the December contract price to rise.

- Shortly thereafter, there is a rumor that Russia is about to make some large-scale purchases of wheat on the world market, and this causes the price to rise. A couple of days later, the rumor appears unfounded and the price again drops.

- Word then comes out of Washington, DC, that some senators from wheat-producing states are going to push for higher price supports in the coming year; so the price increases.

- Later, word comes out that the senators from the cotton producing states are opposing the higher wheat supports unless something is also done for the cotton growers, so the price of wheat declines.

- Then, a government report indicates a worsening inflation picture and, as people rush to buy things, the price of wheat increases.

- A seriously deteriorating situation is revealed in the U.S. balance of payments, indicating a declining U.S. dollar relative to currencies overseas. This makes U.S. products cheaper for foreign customers, so they buy U.S. wheat instead of buying from Canada, Argentina or Australia. This boosts the price of Chicago wheat.

These are a few examples of the myriad of factors that affect the price over a period of time. If the price actually does increase, as our speculator expected, it is because the net effect of all the factors put upward pressure on the price.

And, of course, it is quite possible that the price goes the wrong way after a speculator entered a position on wheat. If the initial move was significant, say $.15 to $.20 per bushel, the loss on the contract would exceed the margin requirement. If the speculator did not close his trade quickly, and/or didn't have sufficient excess margin, the trade would be closed at a significant loss.

You can see from the complexity of the factors influencing the price why there is considerable interest in pursuing "technical" analysis as opposed to, or in addition to, "fundamental" analysis. It could be extremely difficult to both keep track of fundamental factors as given above, and to interpret what their affect would be upon the price. Technical analysis methods, such as those given in this book, attempt to infer the expected behavior of the price from the data supplied by the market itself—price changes, trading volume, changes in open interest, volatility, etc. After all, it is the net effect of all those fundamental factors that is determining the market behavior.

THE SIZE OF THE MARKETS

It is interesting to contemplate the magnitude of the value of commodities traded on the markets each day. Most people are familiar with the workings of the New York Stock Exchange, and accept it as being the largest securities market in the world. There, stocks of the worlds corporations are traded in daily dollar amounts that almost defy comprehension. Yet there are several individual commodities which, by *themselves,* account for dollar volume greater than the aggregate dollar volume of all stocks traded on the NYSE.

The average turnover on the NYSE currently runs about 150,000,000 shares a day, at an average share price of about $30. That is a total dollar value of $4,500,000,000—that's four and a half billion. This exceeds the dollar volume of wheat, which may be $300 million a day, but the aggregate of wheat, corn and soybeans may run about the same as the NYSE dollar volume.

The big trading currently is in the financial futures markets. U.S. treasury bond futures may trade 250 to 300 thousand contracts per day. With each contract representing $100,000 worth of bonds, this is $25- to $30 billion a day in bond value traded. Eurodollars futures commonly trade over $200 billion per day. This is over 40 times the dollar volume of the NYSE.

If you prefer trading the stock market, the commodities market can accommodate you there as well. Stock traders can leverage their action by trading the stock index futures which are keyed to movement of major stock indices; S&P 500, NYSE composite, Value Line, and the Major Market Index. The dollar value represented by trades of the S&P 500 futures alone is around $5 billion.

Appendix B

Generalized Mathematical Formulations

■　■　■

Most of the mathematical formulations provided in the preceding chapters were given in terms of the specific context in which they were being used. For example, an indicator contained a term referred to as "yesterday's," or a summation was referred to in terms of a specific period of time. These formulas are also applicable to weekly or monthly data, or for a different set of cycles over different intervals. The more generalized formulations are given here for those who wish to apply, or tailor, them to other uses.

Reference is made to the applicable section in which they are used, and reference should be made back to that section for more discussion.

Section 1.6 Using the Cycles:

The generalized form for the summation of harmonic cycles of different periods and amplitudes is:

$$P = \overline{P}_m + \Sigma_1^{m-1} A_n \sin\Theta_n$$

where: $\overline{P}_m$ = centered average over the period of the longest cycle, T_m,

$\quad\quad A_n$ = cycle amplitude,

$\quad\quad \Theta_n$ = time point in each cycle,

$$= 2\pi\left(\frac{\tau_n}{T_n} - 1\right)$$

$\quad\quad \tau_n$ = the number of days since the beginning of the cycle,

$\quad\quad T_n$ = cycle period,

$\quad\quad$ and, n, simply denotes the cycle of a given period.

Section 2.4 The Many Uses of Averages:

The Simple Average.

For a string of numbers a,b,c, . . . m, the average, A, is the summation of all the numbers, N_n, divided by the number of numbers, m:

$$A = \frac{\Sigma_1^m N_n}{m}$$

or, as an example, for just four numbers,

$$A = \frac{N_1 + N_2 + N_3 + N_4}{4}$$

We can simplify the computation of the average and avoid having to add up all the numbers each time by using the recursive technique; i.e., subtracting the first number (oldest) and adding the last (newest). For the next interval, the example above becomes:

$$A_{new} = \frac{N_1 + N_2 + N_3 + N_4 - N_1 + N_5}{4}$$

or since the first four numbers in the numerator were already added for the previous average, A_{old}, we can multiply the old average by four, add the newest number and subtract oldest and again divide by four:

$$A_{new} = \frac{4A_{old} + (N_5 - N_1)}{4}$$

Using the recursive property and stating it in a mathematically general way, for any interval, n:

$$A_n = \frac{mA_{n-1} + (N_n - N_{n-m})}{m}$$

The Weighted Average:

A weighted average of a series of numbers, N, with their respective weighting factors, w, is given by:

$$A_w = \frac{w_1N_1 + w_2N_2 \cdots w_mN_m}{\Sigma_{n=1}^{n=m} w_n}$$

The Exponential Average

The exponential moving average is a mathematical expression of a filter as used in the parlance of electronics. The name comes from the way in which the response to an input is described at subsequent intervals.

This filter is simply described as one in which the value at a subsequent interval is a fraction times the new data sample added to one minus the fraction (its complement) times the old value. The fraction is called a "smoothing factor" (which we will denote by the Greek alpha, α), and the formula is written as:

$$EA_{new} = \alpha P_{new} + (1 - \alpha)EA_{old}$$

The exponential moving average theoretically includes all previous data with exponentially decreasing weight. This type of average is recursive and its generalized expression is:

$$EA_n = \alpha N_n + (1 - \alpha)EA_{n-1}$$

A way to characterize a filter is by determining its response to an input. An example of the response of this filter to a step-function input shows how it got its name of "exponential" average. Consider the step function input of p as shown on the diagram. For this simple case the response at time zero is:

$$EA_0 = \alpha P$$

since there is no previous value. At subsequent intervals:

$$EA_1 = \alpha P + (1 - \alpha)\alpha P$$
$$EA_2 = \alpha P + (1 - \alpha) [\alpha P + (1 - \alpha)\alpha P]$$

and so on. By factoring out an αP, the general form is:

$$EA_n = \alpha P[1 + (1 - \alpha) + (1 - \alpha)^2 + (1 - \alpha)^3 + ... (1 - \alpha)^n]$$

A typical response is shown by the stepped line in the diagram. Larger values of alpha respond more quickly, and smaller values, more slowly.

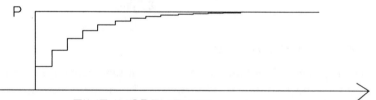

TIME INCREMENTS

From mathematics we know that for alpha less than one, the series:

$$(1 - \alpha) + (1 - \alpha)^2 + (1 - \alpha)^3 + \cdots (1 - \alpha)^n$$

is convergent and converges to:

$$\frac{(1 - \alpha)}{\alpha}$$

and by substituting this back into the equation for the series and simplifying, we get back to our original form.

It has become known as an average because averages are used for the same function—that of filtering the higher frequency variations from market data. This particular mathematical form of filter is very useful in market analysis because it is recursive and simple to calculate, and it is forward weighted, i.e., it gives more emphasis to recent data.

Section 2.6 The Reactivity Factor:

The market reactivity indicator incorporates the price range and trading volume for a particular period by using an aspect ratio:

$$\text{aspect ratio} = \frac{high - low}{volume} = \frac{R}{V}$$

For this ratio to act relative to a given market, or to a particular time period, it needs to be normalized to the average range and volume taken over a number of periods. The normalized aspect ratio, f, is given by:

$$f = \frac{R/\overline{R}}{V/\overline{V}}$$

where: R = range in the period
V = total volume for the period
$\overline{R}$ = average period range over recent past
$\overline{V}$ = average period volume over recent past

The aspect factor will range around 1.0. You can see that a larger than usual range for usual volume will make f larger than 1.0. Values of f larger than 1.0 indicate strongly trending markets and values much less than 1.0 indicate consolidation. It becomes a measure of market behavior.

By multiplying the momentum, M, by the aspect factor taken over the same time period as the momentum, we get an oscillating indicator, the "market reactivity factor," ρ:

$$\rho = f{\cdot}M$$

where f is computed over the same period as the momentum.

The general expression for the market reactivity, computed at each interval for a period covering a number of intervals, m, is:

$$\rho = \frac{R/\overline{R}}{V/\overline{V}} (P_n - P_{n-m})$$

where the price, Pn, is the midpoint price for the current interval, and Pn-mis the price midpoint m intervals ago.

The range, R, is the total range between the highest high and the lowest low price over the period:

$$R = P_{max} - P_{min}$$

and the volume is:

$$V = \Sigma^n_{n-m} = nV_i$$

The average period range and volume, R and V, are computed as trailing exponential averages of the range and volume. The smoothing constant is computed as its approximate equivalence to n intervals, where n covers three to four periods, e.g.:

$$\alpha = \frac{2}{3.5 \cdot n \cdot m + 1}$$

Section 2.7 Monitoring Money Flow:

The basic measure of money flow, MF, is:

$$MF = C \cdot V(M_n - M_{n-1})\left(1 \pm \frac{2|\Delta|}{I}\right)$$

where: C = dollar value of 1-point move
        V = trading volume
        M = daily mean price
        Δ = change in open interest
        I = the larger of today's or yesterday's open interest

The | | around the delta indicates absolute value; i.e., always positive whether the change in open interest is up or down. The + or - in the last term is + if the mean price, M, has gone up or - if the price has gone down.

In this form, this *MF* parameter is a large number and erratic. Once again, to tame the variation, we use an exponential average. And we can get the value to be about the same as the price by using a scaling factor. In the smoothed adjusted form for any interval, *n*, we have:

$$MF_n^s = \frac{MF_{n-1}^s + \alpha(MF_n - MF_{n-1}^2)}{K}$$

The superscript *s* is used to denote the smoothed value which is the only form we will use, and so we will revert to just calling it *MF*.

The typical smoothing constant, alpha, is 0.1 and the scaling factor, *K*, is about 100,000. Although the dollar value per point has a given value, it can be combined with the scaling factor and a value selected to give a suitable range.

Section 2.8 Additional Indicators for Stock Index Futures:

The Issues Index

A useful way to use the number of advancing and declining issues is to express the net number of advancers or decliners as a percentage of total issues traded:

$$N = 100 \cdot \frac{A - D}{A + D + U}$$

The denominator is total issues traded; i.e., advances and declines and unchanged. This parameter is erratic and is tamed by taking a 12-day running exponential average (0.15 smoothing constant) to obtain the issues index:

$$I_n = I_{n-1} + 0.15 \cdot (N_n - I_{n-1})$$

A Good Over-bought/Over-sold Indicator

A good longer term (50-100 day) OB-OS indicator is the 30-day summation A/D ratio:

$$OB/OS = \frac{\Sigma_{-30}^n A_i}{\Sigma_{-30}^n D_i}$$

or simply summing the last 30 days of the number of advancing issues and dividing by the sum of the last 30 days of the number of declining issues.

Plurality

The plurality index is based simply on the running total of the net number of issues advancing or declining,

$$p = \Sigma(A_n - D_n)$$

This basic concept, first applied by Paul Dysart, is applied in different forms to make it more well behaved and useful. The basic application is generally the same, i.e., a leading (or divergent) indicator presaging sentiment change.

Although Dysart used a 15-day summation, the more commonly used form is a continuing summation:

$$AD_n = AD_{n-1} + (A - D)_n$$

and is called the advance-decline line, or AD line. It is a measure of the "breadth" of market participation.

TRIN

A popular, very short term index indicator of the market sentiment is the Arms index (developed by Richard Arms) or also commonly referred to as the TRIN. This indicator is computed as a combination of the advancing and declining issues and the corresponding advancing and declining volume.

$$TRIN = \frac{A/D}{V_a/V_d}$$

It is a ratio of ratios and indicates a concentration of volume in the advancing or declining stocks, indicating bullish or bearish sentiment respectively.

The TRIN is best used as an indicator of intra-day strength. A value of 1.0 is neutral with lower values bullish and higher values bearish. Values of about 0.75 or less indicate strength, and values over about 1.3 indicate weakness. A value of about 0.5 or less after an hour of trading gives a high probability of a strong rally day.

It is also used as a 10-day trailing average for longer term indication of market sentiment. When the 10-day average value gets to 0.8 or below it indicates "over bought" conditions, and one can expect a sell-off. Usually the sell-off doesn't really get underway until the 10-day TRIN works its way back up to around 0.9 or 1.0. Similarly, values of 1.2 or greater indicate an "oversold" condition.

Section 4.3 Computing the Stop-loss Point:

Compute the average daily range, ADR, as:

$$ADR_n = ADR_{n-1} + 0.13(R_n - ADR_{n-1})$$

where R is today's price range and n is the day number. For simplicity, assume tomorrow's midpoint is the exponentially smoothed midpoint for today:

$$M_{n+1} = \overline{M}_{n-1} + \alpha(M_n - \overline{M}_{n-1})$$

A typical value for alpha of 0.4 works fine. Then compute the standard deviation in the daily range using the last 15 days of the daily range data.

Now, we can compute a reasonable stop-loss point for tomorrow's session. If we have a long position, the long stop point is:

$$STP_l = M_{n+1} - \left(\frac{ADR_n}{2} + K \cdot \sigma_n\right)$$

and a short position stop point is:

$$STP_l = M_{n+1} + \left(\frac{ADR_n}{2} + K \cdot \sigma_n\right)$$

The constant, k, is a multiplier for the standard deviation to adjust the probability for tomorrow's expected range to stay within the limits. This is best determined empirically by examining data for the commodity you are trading and choosing a value which keeps the stop point just out of range of the typical pull-backs in price with the trend that you are trading. Typically, a value around 2.0 works well.

If your trade is correct, there is a high probability that tomorrow's price will not go against you beyond the stop point. If it does, you should certainly re-examine your indicators and/or exit the position.

INDEX

SPREADSHEET TEMPLATES

***READY-TO-USE
WORKSHEETS WITH
MORE THAN 6 MONTHS
PAST DATA BUILT IN;
CURRENT CONTRACT
READY TO TRADE***

Worksheet files for LOTUS 1-2-3, EXCEL and compatible spreadsheet software are available on disk for PC compatibles. They are ready-to-use worksheets including all the necessary equations, graphics and spreadsheet maintenance MACROS for trading with the ***Market Reactivity System***. Each is tailored to the cycle characteristics of the particular commodity. Each template order also includes setup of a practice worksheet for familiarization and trading of historical data.

One commodity	$195.00
Add up to three @	115.00 each
Add four or more @	95.00 each

HISTORICAL DATA

Daily data from 1986 to present that is in a format ready to import into the practice/study spreadsheet. Includes high, low, close, volume and change in open interest. Also includes up to 15 years of weekly midpoint data.

Each $29.00, Five or more $24.00 each

- -

ORDER FORM

Please send me the Templates and Data as checked below. Enclosed is a check or money order for total due.

WINDOWS: 1-2-3 ❑   EXCEL ❑
DOS: 1-2-3 ❑

Templates	*Data*		*Amount*
Coffee	❑	❑	_____
Copper	❑	❑	_____
Cotton	❑	❑	_____
Eurodollars	❑	❑	_____
Live Hogs	❑	❑	_____
Natural Gas	❑	❑	_____
Yen	❑	❑	_____
CBT Wheat	❑	❑	_____
S&P 500	❑	n/a	_____
Total			_____

Name_____

Address_____

City/State/ZIP_____

Phone _____

Send order to: ***AL Ventures***, P.O. Box 53, Point Richmond, CA, 94807

Please allow up to 2–3 weeks for delivery (faster for cashiers check or M.O.). There can be no assurance or guarantee that trading with this system will be successful. Although potential gains can be substantial, the risk of loss can also be high. You should carefully consider whether trading is suitable for you.

About the Author

■ ■ ■

Al Gietzen has traded the commodity markets and done technical analysis for more than ten years. He trades managed accounts, provides consulting service on trading with the *Market Reactivity System* and gives an occasional lecture to investment groups and at trading seminars. He is also an Adjunct faculty member at the JFK University School of Management and is the Executive Director of a non-profit organization which provides recreation and athletic programs for people with disabilities.

His past achievements include development of a successful selection system for growth company investment. He owned and managed a successful real estate program, led the establishment of two small businesses and has done investment management consulting.

Mr. Gietzen has a masters degree in engineering from Stanford University and has extensive background in engineering analysis, project management, manufacturing management, and management of domestic and international marketing. This work involved complex technical systems and required extensive travel and working with people of many different cultural backgrounds.

He has authored numerous technical reports and has presented papers at national and international conferences. He has also served on a U.N. agency committee which developed guidelines for research facilities in developing countries.